"The nonprofit arts sector can no longer
and wishful thinking. Entrepreneurial Arts
roadmap for arts leaders ready to embrace business-minded, revenue-generating strategies that ensure long-term sustainability. This book challenges the status quo and offers the tools we need to reimagine the future of our field."

—**Michael J. Bobbitt**, executive arts leader and playwright

"I teach a graduate course in arts leadership and can see the applicability of this book directly connected to the principles that are part of my syllabus. As such, the authors demonstrate a practical application of a process that entails the cultivation of a team of critical thinkers and creative problem-solvers to propel an organization forward."

"The alliance of theory and practice is a model that can be an inspiration for emerging leaders in arts administration. It could also provide a catalyst to generate a new paradigm of thinking for seasoned leaders who need rejuvenation."

—**Dr. Gail Humphries**, dean emerita, Stephens College, USA and College of Fellows of the American Theatre, USA; professor emerita, American University, USA

"I've witnessed firsthand as Imagination Stage adapted and intrepidly entered new business markets, while authentically honoring foundational values over decades under Bonnie Fogel's leadership. As nonprofit leaders, we are, inherently, entrepreneurs with a societal purpose. This book will inspire others who seek to maximize the impact of their nonprofits."

—**Jose Antonio Tijerino**, president and CEO, Hispanic Heritage Foundation; board member, Independent Sector, board member, Imagination Stage 2010–21

"Entrepreneurial Arts and Culture Leadership *offers a unique tale of creation, expansion, collaboration, and ultimately the success of a nonprofit theater. The extraordinary 40-year history not only gives definition to entrepreneurial leadership in the arts context but also provides the tools needed for one to develop such a leadership practice. Arts leaders, board members, and students will benefit from this wealth of knowledge as they advance their own successful and sustainable arts organizations."*

—**Dr. Kate Keeney**, associate professor, arts leadership and entrepreneurship, University of Maryland, USA

Entrepreneurial Arts and Cultural Leadership

Jane ~

Thank you for your entrepreneurial leadership, and guidance and your friendship and support through the years. It made such a difference.

♡ always

Bernice

The photo represents the constantly shifting sands the nonprofit arts leader must navigate. These dunes are challenging to traverse and just when you think you have scaled them, the pattern changes – as must your journey.

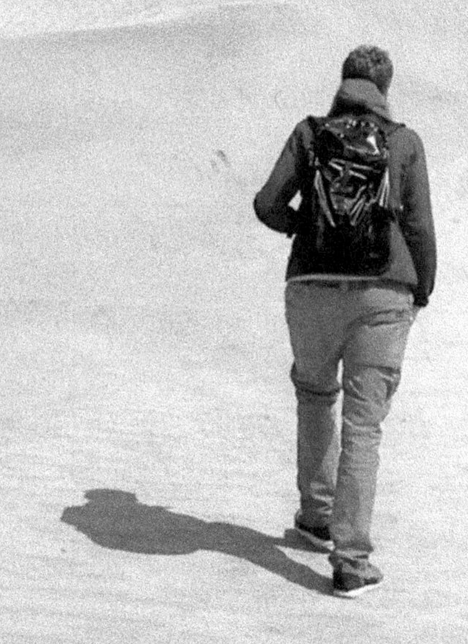

Entrepreneurial Arts and Cultural Leadership

Traits of Success in Nonprofit Theatre

Bonnie Fogel and Brett Ashley Crawford

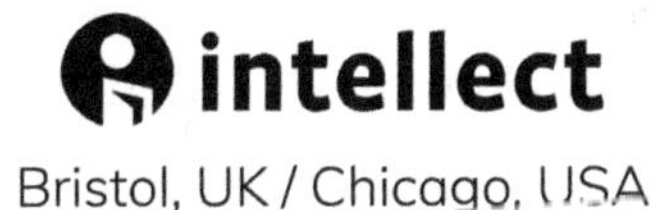
Bristol, UK / Chicago, USA

First published in the UK in 2025 by
Intellect, The Mill, Parnall Road, Fishponds, Bristol, BS16 3JG, UK

First published in the USA in 2025 by
Intellect, The University of Chicago Press, 1427 E. 60th Street,
Chicago, IL 60637, USA

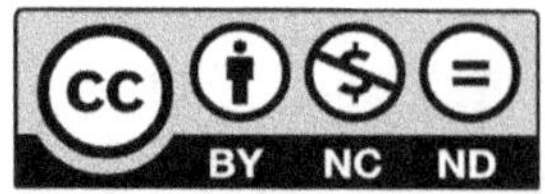

A catalogue record for this book is available from
the British Library.

Copy editor: MPS Limited
Cover designer: Tanya Montefusco
Cover and frontispiece image: The Dunes in Swakopmund, Namibia. Courtesy of Bonnie Fogel, with creative support from Samantha Sonnet.
Production manager: Sophia Munyengeterwa and Tian Greaves
Typesetter: MPS Limited

Hardback ISBN 978-1-83595-119-4
Paperback ISBN 978-1-83595-122-4
ePDF ISBN 978-1-83595-121-7
ePUB ISBN 978-1-83595-120-0

This is a peer-reviewed publication.

Contents

Figures

Acknowledgments

This book would not have been possible without the support and contributions of so many people. We are deeply grateful to Jessica Lovett, Sophia Munyengeterwa, Tian Greaves and the editing team at Intellect Books for believing in the book and shepherding us through the project. We are also grateful to those who offered guidance and feedback on various drafts of the work, including Pam Roberts, Gail Humphries and Haylee Massaro. And our cover image would not have been complete without the artistic touch of Samantha Sonnet. And we both have an individual network of friends, family and colleagues without whom this would have never been possible.

For Brett: First and foremost, I am eternally grateful to Sandy Murphy for her patience and support throughout the writing of this book. Without her, nothing would have been possible. And I would like to thank Richard Bradbury, Kate Bryer and Janet Stanford for bringing me into the BAPA/Imagination Stage family as a stage manager. The impact and spirit of their work confirmed for me that theatre really can and does change the world. And a magnificent thank you to Bonnie for inviting me to join the administrative side of the business. A move that was one of the most important moments in my life and career. Our partnership has continued into the writing of this book. In writing it, I have been reminded of what great things our collaboration had and is again bringing to life.

For Bonnie: My thanks to my teachers at Lyme Regis Grammar School, United Kingdom, who showed me that creativity can make up for a lack of academic skills; to Marks & Spencer from whom I learned Entrepreneurialism 101; to Bethesda Academy of Performing Arts and Imagination Stage board members and staff associates for encouraging me to fly and being the "wind beneath my wings"; and especially to Marcia Smith and Janet Stanford for having the courage to take a risk with me. And, ultimately, heartfelt thanks to Brett for her immediate enthusiasm and commitment to this project. Deep gratitude to Sally, Adela, Judy, Lynn and Pat for their forever friendship and to Dick, Sarah, Jessica and David Fogel, Vicky Unwin, and Matthew Killian for unwavering family support from the beginning of my entrepreneurial journey. And finally, to "the little boys" – Aden, Leon and Noah – for representing our best possible future.

Introduction: Why Is Entrepreneurship Critical in Arts Leadership?

We are what we do; excellence then is not an act, but a habit.

—Aristotle

Introduction

Entrepreneurial Arts and Cultural Leadership: Traits of Success in Nonprofit Theatre offers emerging and established arts and nonprofit leaders a deep understanding of how to establish an entrepreneurial mindset. This will allow them to adapt quickly to opportunities while meeting the considerable demands of managing the complex operations of an arts and cultural enterprise.

The book meets the global need to create a "new business model" in the face of changing global economic and social conditions. We centered the story on a real business case study and included the theories, strategies and tactics to not only achieve but also maintain success as a nonprofit. *Entrepreneurial Arts and Cultural Leadership* serves those working in nonprofit organizations and those in the classroom learning how to lead. It is organized in an accessible model offering six core traits that we contend define success in entrepreneurial nonprofit leadership.

The arts and cultural sector is big business. In 2022, nonprofit arts and culture organizations generated $151.7 billion in economic activity, $73.3 billion in spending by the organizations, and an additional $78.4 billion in event-related spending by their audiences, according to Americans for the Arts' 6th annual Arts and Economic Prosperity survey. The report notes that "the impact of this economic activity is far-reaching, supporting 2.6 million jobs, generating $29.1 billion in tax revenue, and providing $101 billion in personal income to residents."[1]

And, the problems facing nonprofit organizations across the globe are equally big. These include shifting audience patterns, a lower response from donors, and shifting priorities in foundations, corporations, and governmental support systems.

As we write, arts and cultural organizations are still adapting to the world left behind by the COVID-19 pandemic. Some headlines are dire, noting organizations closing or suspending operations to develop a new "business model."

2020 introduced significant changes to the world's business and social fabric. The nonprofit arts, especially performing arts, have been greatly impacted by the highest unemployment rate during the peak of the pandemic to the slow, inconsistent return of patrons.[2] Internally, nonprofit arts organizations had to address often long-overdue adaptations to the inclusive and accessible practices demanded by their communities, including equitable pay scales, diversity, inclusion and access on stage, staffs, and boards.

Consequently, many nonprofit arts organizations are now less viable; many have gone out of business; and most are struggling to adopt new post-pandemic practices that promote a new culture in their organization. **We contend that those organizations that have survived are led by social entrepreneurs who were ahead of the curve and able to adapt quickly.**

For the arts, the pandemic did not cause the problems but instead exacerbated deeper-seated issues. For instance, audience numbers in the performing arts in the United States have been decreasing for decades. Donations may have been strong for many, but the amounts were often provided by fewer individuals. And the social justice movement began well before 2020, starting conversations in governments and foundations about funding priorities. Nonprofit arts organizations experienced ten years of change in less than two years, leaving them reeling, and exhausted from the uncharted territory.

Comparatively few nonprofits grow year-over-year, meet their mission, support their vision and bring new services to their ever-changing communities – those that do are led by leaders with an entrepreneurial business approach.

This book offers answers for those who are struggling and know that change is needed. *Entrepreneurial Arts and Cultural Leadership* differs from others in that it looks closely at one nonprofit organization, Imagination Stage, that, under one leader, moved through five evolutions, also known as business pivots, across 40 years, reaching more individuals and creating a greater impact at each change. It details specific entrepreneurial traits in detail that can lead to success. Imagination Stage consistently embraced an entrepreneurial approach that helped the organization to persevere even when times were especially difficult.

Entrepreneurial Arts and Cultural Leadership complements the arts management and arts leadership textbooks in the market that demonstrate the standard structures and assumptions. While it underscores core theories at the start of each chapter, its power comes from the demonstration of how to be entrepreneurial and nimbly adapt to new opportunities while developing a thriving nonprofit leadership system.

Entrepreneurial Arts and Cultural Leadership provides a toolkit for the nonprofit leader or aspirant: it's for students of nonprofit arts management looking to strengthen leadership skills, and it's also for those struggling to support their sagging nonprofits. *Entrepreneurial Arts and Cultural Leadership: Traits of Success in Nonprofit Theatre* assumes that the nonprofit, imagined or realized, has an excellent vision and mission that fills a unique need in the community. The remaining challenge is ensuring the nonprofit survives, thrives and is holistically stable.

Entrepreneurial Arts and Cultural Leadership suggests that arts leaders meet the demands of our changing world – a world of divided ideas, wealth imbalance, social unrest and climate change by adopting entrepreneurial practices, now.

Despite an abundance of resources:

- **Thousands of well-intentioned nonprofits with great visions and missions go out of business every year due to ineffective management practices.**
- **Thousands of well-intentioned nonprofits with great visions and missions do NOT go out of business every year but exist in a perpetual struggle between success and failure which, saps them of energy and ensures that they do not meet their potential.**

Most of these "resources" are provided by academics with no lived experience in the nonprofit world and most cling to traditional beliefs that vision, mission and excellent practice are all it takes to ensure success in the nonprofit world. Nothing could be further from the truth.

Entrepreneurial Arts and Cultural Leadership satisfies a global need for an educational and practical approach that complements grounding academic principles of nonprofit management with a "real world" business approach complete with strategies and tactics designed to build and sustain a viable nonprofit. *Entrepreneurial Arts and Cultural Leadership* is a needed classroom text ***and*** an accessible step-by-step guide to the six traits that the authors contend define success in nonprofit management.

Why We Wrote This Book

In 2012, Brett transitioned from Imagination Stage to teaching at Carnegie Mellon University. The MA in arts management focuses on arts, analytics and action – with a pedagogy that focuses on the future, not the past. Once there, she realized that the core examples offered in standard textbooks were often teaching models from the past that were increasingly ill-suited to address today's challenges.

Furthermore, as someone who deeply believes in systems theory, she teaches a framework of how to create a culture of success with tools and measures. Many of her core examples were from her work and her understanding of the success of Imagination Stage. Throughout the last decade, Bonnie has been repeatedly asked to mentor emerging arts and cultural leaders. Again, she used her experience in establishing a culture and working through an entrepreneurial mindset as a norm for success. *Entrepreneurial Arts and Cultural Leadership* represents their discussions and practice.

What You'll Find in the Book

Every chapter begins by offering a framework of core concepts in the field that provide a context to better understand the examples provided from the case study. The Case Study section tells the story of the practice of entrepreneurial leadership at Imagination Stage through in-depth examples. Quotes from organization stakeholders are offered throughout in sidebars. Each chapter concludes with a "Wrap" and some discussion questions oriented to levels of experience and flexible to your context.

Case Study Method

The case study has become renowned as a means for teaching in business. *Harvard Business Review* offers a trove of case studies used for teaching in business schools across the world. The power of the case study is the opportunity to learn from others' experiences. This is also the power of the arts, particularly those art forms grounded in storytelling, from literature to dance to theatre.

The traditional "case study" in textbooks or in case study work, however, tends to offer an in-depth look at a moment in time. These studies present a case for discussion of how a company solved a specific problem through a selection of strategies and/or tactics. Our book offers a deeper model for learning through a 40-year case study, a case study and history of one organization that provides a framework for success through repeated practice, in fact a mindset, of entrepreneurship. (See "Appendix A for The Origin Story")

Dates and Terminology

The era discussed focuses on the founding of the organization from 1979 to 2021.

The term nonprofit is used throughout to talk about the structures and the status of Imagination Stage. The US not-for-profit sector has 29 different types of nonprofits. The 501c3 is characterized as those organizations that are exempt from taxes due to a 501c3 designated mission and purpose and that the organization may accept tax-deductible donations from donors of all types. While we might say that it is a mission-focused enterprise, the tax designation frames it as a charitable nonprofit.[3]

Overview of Arts Management and Leadership

Before understanding the entrepreneurial twist, an introduction to the standard management literature is of value; it is impossible in a few short pages to accomplish what many books cover in great depth; see the Bibliography for a list of suggested books on these topics. A nonprofit enterprise is a business similar to any other business. In fact, some leaders say that the only difference is the tax status since, in the United States, both businesses are structured as corporations. And, while that is perhaps true at the surface, that tax status comes with a significant impact on the way the nonprofit is run. Unlike the profit and market-driven goals of the for-profit sector, nonprofits must direct their activities to achieve a mission that impacts society. Furthermore, a nonprofit requires a board of directors or trustees composed of volunteers, **not** individuals compensated for their work, paid in cash or as stockholders of the company.

Arts and cultural nonprofits have an additional layer of complexity. They have a charitable status because of their social good mission and their impact on the community. This gives them access to contributed income to support their work. Unlike a social service, animal welfare or environmental nonprofit that focuses on programs that support the community and only generate income from contributions, the arts and culture business includes, in fact often exists, to offer what for many has become significant earned income programs. For example, ballet companies charge tuition for younger students or general fitness programs for the public as well as ballet performances with tickets sold to audiences. Earned income complicates the argument for the charitable position of the organization. How, might one ask, is a top-tier nonprofit theatre experience different than a commercial enterprise? It is not at the surface. A performance is mounted, tickets are offered and paid for, and an audience attends. **It is, however, created with a different purpose and impact.** And the proceeds serve the mission, not the pockets of the investors.

For those wanting to manage arts and cultural organizations, many textbooks address core practices. William Byrnes has created four editions of

Management and the Arts,[4] Ellen Rosewall's *Arts Management: Uniting Arts and Audiences in the Twenty-First Century*[5] is on its second edition, to name a few. In addition, a plethora of materials addresses best practices in particular art forms, from *The Cycle* by Michael Kaiser to *Performing Arts Management* by Tobie Stein[6,7] to *Museum Operations* by Samantha Chmelik[8] and a myriad of others addressing theatres, orchestras, dance companies, galleries, festivals, etc. (See Bibliography)

Textbooks on arts leadership are also abundant. And, entrepreneurship as a subset of arts management is not new but often targeted at artists and artpreneurs, from Miriam Schulman[9] to Lukas De Beer[10] who claims to have coined the term "artpreneurs." None explicitly focuses on entrepreneurship for nonprofit organizations and their leaders. (See Bibliography)

The Nonprofit Entrepreneurship Approach

In the **for-profit world**, an entrepreneur is someone who **creates a new product or service** and then markets that product or service to make a profit. While this may sound simple enough, the entrepreneurial approach is usually associated with risk. Conversely, a non-entrepreneurial, typical business, approach maximizes process and systems and minimizes risk.

Nonprofit **leaders are – or at least began as – inherently entrepreneurial. Such institutions** are typically established by someone who sees a social need (as opposed to a product need) and then acts on it, **despite potential financial and reputational risks.** Nonprofit entrepreneurship is often referred to as "**social entrepreneurship**" – where the reward is not financial but societal.

If you take the definition of entrepreneurial thought leader, Eric Reis, who explains in *The Lean Startup*[11] that entrepreneurs create programs against unknown circumstances, it follows that nonprofit leaders are genetically entrepreneurial. When we create a new play, a new exhibition or even exhibit an established work in a new community, we take a significant risk. We don't know if the audience will come. We don't know if donors or foundations will find the offer compelling.

Nonprofit entrepreneurial leaders are:

- **Visionary** – they identify opportunities in the nonprofit's community,
- **Creative and innovative** – they imagine new ways to provide new opportunities through innovative programming and services,
- "**People**" people – they engage the right people to help them,

- **Market savvy** – they can "read" the market to determine what will sell,
- **Promoters/advocates** – they know how to successfully promote products/services, and
- **Effective risk managers** – they have the administrative capabilities to manage innovation and financial and reputational risk.

We reference these traits in every chapter to align the theories and examples described and discussed to the traits above.

Many people align entrepreneurship with the idea of the "start-up" but it is increasingly recognized as a mindset of innovation and leadership. The core concept of entrepreneurship is embedded in the framework of the *Blue Ocean Strategy* by W. Chan Kim and Renée Mauborgne, where they explain that a Blue Ocean is "the simultaneous pursuit of differentiation and low cost to open up a new market space and create new demand. It is about creating and capturing uncontested market space, thereby making the competition irrelevant." This is different from the Red Ocean strategy of finding your unique value in a traditional marketplace, for example, starting a theatre that focuses on new plays in a community that has several other theatres presenting Broadway musicals, small musicals and the standard restaging of established canon plays.[12]

Imagination Stage under Bonnie's leadership created multiple Blue Oceans, consistently developing markets where none existed before; examples you will discover throughout the book include creating an arts education enterprise based in theatre where few existed (1979) and expanding from there by creating a product for students with access and inclusion needs. The mission inspired the pursuit with the realization that there was an entire population of young people not being served. The organization then expanded from arts education to a professional theatre, adding this product line and a new market of new audiences to serve. Twenty years later, after seeing the genre in Europe, Imagination Stage was one of the first in the United States to create a professional theatre product for very young children (ages 2–4) and their parents; the venture was launched to immediate market success. And when arts education was being cut in schools, Imagination Stage developed tools and residency training programs for arts integration ahead of the market that is now saturated and structured. And, in its most recent evolution, Imagination Stage uncovered how it could support a population of young people who had not previously been served – youth who, from global and local circumstances, were in need of new tools for recovery from life trauma.

Entrepreneurs indulge in "risky business" that is actually a Blue Ocean.

— Brett Ashley Crawford, teaching professor, Carnegie Mellon University; Imagination Stage managing director, 2006–12

Successful entrepreneurs listen to their customers. Nonprofits are no different, but their customers are the community, their audience and their donors. It is a complex system to manage, which is why substantial literature addresses the basics of arts and cultural management and leadership.

As has been proven in leadership studies, most people are not born leaders but learn how to be a leader developing skills and habits over time. This holds true for entrepreneurial leadership. The secret of success for entrepreneurial leadership is the practice of lifelong learning. While Brett started her practice through a path of higher education, Bonnie developed hers by taking advantage of the resources around her:

> I joke that I earned my MFA – not at Yale – but from all those arts management courses I took in my early nonprofit career days at just about any free, or very inexpensive, professional nonprofit training opportunity. I attended many in-person workshops and found that while there was a great diversity of organization size in the room, the issues are the same, they are just on a different point of the spectrum. So, I always left with many new ideas and practices.
>
> Family beach vacations were when I read books on nonprofit management and for-profit business success stories. Our small overburdened staff probably dreaded my return knowing all the new ideas for our growing business that would ensue. As I increased my own knowledge, I encouraged staff to read avidly and across genres, particularly biographies of leaders. Newspapers, magazines, podcasts, all provided the necessary context critical to planning, policy and practice.

And we both learned that **community and civic group engagement** offers opportunities that are often overlooked by nonprofit leaders. While a nonprofit business has core differences from a for-profit, we all learn from each other. Bonnie prioritized membership in her local Chamber of Commerce amongst others. **The return on investment turned out to be exceptional.** She learned much about the value of large boards, large committees and board and member engagement; she modeled many of Imagination Stage's board practices on her experiences there.

How to Read This Book

What you will find here is something completely different from the standard text or nonprofit arts management book. *Entrepreneurial Arts and Cultural Leadership* offers a deep exploration of one organization to demonstrate how an entrepreneurial mindset, innovation and leadership informed one organization's growth across 40 years. Some, in fact, may want to start their journey by reading "Appendix A: The Origin Story," to get a grounding in the who, what and why of Imagination Stage's history.

We organized the book around six core traits that can be read individually as needed or as a whole from beginning to end. Depending on where you, our reader, find yourself in your entrepreneurial leadership journey will guide your approach. Because we designed the book to be read in sections as needed for workshops, classes or staff meetings, each chapter has some repetition of Imagination Stage's history as needed for the trait discussed. We believe this repetition has value, as it offers different perspectives on the same moment in time, allowing for a deeper understanding of the multi-pronged work of a nonprofit entrepreneurial leader.

Trait 1. The Vision Thing: The Entrepreneurial Leadership Imperative

In this chapter, you will gain a thorough understanding of how an entrepreneurial leader establishes a path to success by seeing the needs of their community and by envisioning the innovations needed to create success. The chapter begins with an understanding of the core concepts and differentiation between mission, vision and values and how these relate to the entrepreneurial, Blue Ocean practice of seeing the need and envisioning the solution. The four-plus evolutions, also known as business pivots, of Imagination Stage, from its founding to the COVID-19 pandemic, are provided with an understanding of the mission-framed opportunities and the entrepreneurial vision that moved the organization into those markets.

Trait 2. It's All About the People: Staff and Board

Nonprofits, particularly arts and cultural nonprofits, are people-driven enterprises. People make or collect or curate the art and organizations' people work to serve individuals in their communities. This chapter offers a framework for finding and working with the best people (staff and board) to do the job. The core theories presented are those that fueled the work at Imagination Stage. The chapter offers experience in how to know and work with like-minded, passionate individuals and explains how as organizations grow and as people change, sometimes it is in the person and organization's best interest to support a separation.

Trait 3. Igniting and Engaging: Entrepreneurial Leadership and the Board

As noted earlier, nonprofit corporations are different from their for-profit peers in that their board is constructed of volunteers who are serving the mission and stewarding the organization for the community's best interest. Boards are a unique but critical subset of people who, when engaged entrepreneurially, can support and expand the work of an entrepreneurial leader. The chapter offers core reasons and legal requirements for the structures and responsibilities of a board. The case study provides the perspective and best practices that supported Imagination Stage's success, especially its dating–proposal–marriage pipeline for board member engagement.

Trait 4. Making the Difference: Partnerships and Community

This chapter offers the frameworks and understanding of the value of partnerships and provides examples of how Imagination Stage worked with community stakeholders to synergistically amplify impact for mutual benefit. From government partners to shared nonprofit programs, partnerships *in* the community outside of the core arts (or nonprofit) activity are critical to the success of Imagination Stage. These partnerships allowed all involved to leverage their best to accomplish more and, quite often, achieve impact and funding in ways never possible alone.

Trait 5. The Power of Your Voice and Advocacy

Many nonprofit organizations view their role in advocacy too narrowly. This chapter explains broader opportunities and perspectives on the role of advocacy in a nonprofit's work and eventual success. Advocacy must be more than an email to a public official in times of crisis, but, rather, a long-term relationship cultivation process that crosses political parties. Imagination Stage case study repeatedly demonstrates how advocacy work and relationships with elected and appointed officials paved the way for the organization that would otherwise have been stifled.

Trait 6. The Entrepreneurial Balance: Risk vs. Opportunity

Entrepreneurial leadership is, like all work in this nonprofit space, risky. This chapter offers lessons on how to balance risk when opportunities arise. The case study provides examples of success, failure, accountability measures and triggers for alternative paths. It also offers a view of an entrepreneurial mindset that allows for change, experimentation and, sometimes, big leaps and a practice of thinking outside the box. The chapter breaks down the risk into three areas: financial, cultural and reputational.

Appendices

The appendices offer history, tactics and tools. They begin with the "origin" story for those interested in how to start an operation and continue with a detailed chronology of the organization. The many people who were critical to the success of the organization across the 40 years are included in a "Who's Who." Finally, several appendices provide tactical "how-tos" and samples of key documents someone can use in their own entrepreneurial leadership practice. These practical documents offer iterations of core concepts discussed in their related *Entrepreneurial Arts and Cultural Leadership* chapter.

Trait 1

The Vision Thing: The Entrepreneurial Leadership Imperative

The only thing worse than being blind is having sight but no vision.

—Helen Keller

Fifty years ago, the nonprofit business differentiated itself from the private, for-profit business sector by creating a mission or vision statement designed to change society in order to create a better world. In fact, mission-focused work is *required* by law for a nonprofit arts and cultural organization. Regardless of your business structure, mission, vision and value statements serve as a managerial tool, increasing effectiveness and providing the boundaries for the work you do.

In fact, Jim Collins explains that:

> A well-conceived vision consists of two major components: *core ideology* and *envisioned future*. Core ideology ... defines what we stand for and why we exist. ... The envisioned future is what we aspire to become, to achieve, to create — something that will require significant change and progress to attain.[13]
>
> —Jim Collins

If a nonprofit is to stand the test of time, it must have a solid and inspiring and unwavering vision. The vision must be easily understood and communicated and embraced by every member of the not-for-profit community: staff associates, board members, and the community of users and stakeholders. Today, to ensure viability, we must work equally hard on ensuring profit since, without sustainability, there is no business, no mission and no vision. Is there a conflict between being an entrepreneurial leader of a nonprofit and the more traditional management approach of doing the work, then hoping, praying and anticipating the money will come? We posit that balancing vision and mission with the market-savvy, entrepreneurial approach provides a dynamic and healthy tension.

We must embrace the tenets of entrepreneurial vision while honoring our social impact mission. On the other end of the leadership spectrum (non-entrepreneurial), non-engaged managers (managers who are not leaders) wear blinders and keep their noses next to the grindstones of their businesses, unaware of new opportunities or imminent challenges. We are distinguishing between managers who are not leaders, leaders who are managers and leaders who are entrepreneurs in this book. A manager uses resources to accomplish a task. A manager-leader focuses on leading a company through a set of actions to accomplish a defined company goal. An entrepreneurial leader stands out as they incorporate a visionary mindset that seeks new opportunities beyond the norms of an industry. Entrepreneurial visionaries:

- are always tweaking their visions; they are alert to the changing world and its needs. They ask their associates: "what is the message here for our business; what does our community need; what can we provide/sell?";
- know they need the right people standing shoulder-to-shoulder with them and are not challenged by those who know more than they do (see Trait 2);
- are always looking at sustainability, at new markets and new cost centers; and
- understand that developing an entrepreneurial habit of mind and engaging the right people is not enough: marketing is all.

Before we explore the entrepreneurial approach and the critical need for a leader who is both a visionary **and** entrepreneurial (which, let's be clear, is not the same thing), it is important to define the core frameworks and practices for establishing a traditional nonprofit organization's mission, vision and values statement and the difference among the three.

In this chapter, we spotlight the entrepreneurial traits identified in the Introduction:

- Visionary – they identify opportunities in the nonprofit's community;
- Market savvy– they can "read" the market to determine if this will sell.

Mission

The mission statement is part of an organization's articles of incorporation and is the distinguishing factor for gaining nonprofit status (501c3). But it is far more than that. It is not simply a slogan on a wall – although often for-profit organizations will lean in on the marketing tagline. A mission statement is a brief, powerful statement of the reason the organization exists.

The mission is the value proposition. What is the value we are offering to our community? The mission statement defines, or at least frames, what the organization will achieve through its programs. The mission should say who you are, what you do, who you serve and why. The why may be implied or tied into the vision, but it is ultimately the impact we will have on the community we serve.

The word choice in your mission statement is incredibly significant. By changing one word, your work and your impact can change. For example, is your organization serving *families* or is it serving *children*? Are you focusing on the power of *storytelling* or *theatre*? While these words have clear overlaps, they will put some people and activities in your rooms and **keep** others out. What are you really trying to **do** and for **whom**?

According to Board Source, the go-to service organization for best practices and training for board development, there are nine characteristics of a mission statement:

- Contains bold, clear, memorable language,
- Conveys the organization's values implicitly if not explicitly,
- Carries emotional and rational impact,
- Uses active verbs,
- Combines a why statement with a what statement,
- Describes the need in positive terms,
- Is succinct,
- Inspires people to join, give, act, serve, learn more, and
- Can be incorporated into marketing and fundraising communications.[14]

Vision

While a mission defines the organization's value proposition – the what, who and why of the work it does, the vision statement expresses how the world will be different from that work in twenty-plus years. The vision is the future state of the organization and the world. If our mission succeeds, what will the world look like, how will those who participate in our programs be changed? For example, if my organization's mission is to solve the problem of homelessness, then the vision statement would reflect the change that will **result when everybody has** a home. For Imagination Stage, for example, the vision of a life changed by our programs is a future where **theatre** experiences are a fundamental aspect

> *There is nothing humble about our vision.*
>
> — Janet Stanford, founding artistic director 1992–2024

of all children's lives, nourishing their creative spirit, inspiring them to embrace the complexity and diversity of their world, and helping them overcome their challenges with both courage and above all creativity. So essentially, **when** all children have access to theatre, **all children will feel creative** and inspired.

Values

Values are part of the triumvirate but function as boundaries to the work, often providing a decision-making framework. They also influence the culture of the organization. For example, if you value your staff, then your policy for surplus funds will include them in its distribution.

The mission, vision and values statement of Imagination Stage, prior to COVID-19, was:

Mission
Imagination Stage produces theatre and arts education programs which nurture, challenge and empower young people of all abilities.

Vision
Imagination Stage envisions a future where theatre experiences are a fundamental aspect of children's lives, nourishing their creative spirit, inspiring them to embrace the complexity and diversity of their world and helping them overcome their challenges with hope, courage and, above all, creativity.

Values
The values of Imagination Stage are informed by a passionate commitment to ensuring that theatre is an essential thread in the fabric of learning and of life. We value:

- *Inclusiveness and diversity by including all artistry, abilities and talent, by welcoming and serving the diversity of our community, and by respecting the diversity of our world in our work.*
- *Investment in the future of young people through our commitment to nurturing their creative and intellectual growth through excellent, innovative theatre and arts education experiences.*
- *Service on behalf of children as we work to use theatre as a way to improve the lives of children in our community regardless of their means or their location.*
- *Our staff associates by cherishing their contributions to the achievement of our important mission and vision.*

The Entrepreneurial Twist

A nonprofit entrepreneurial vision must establish how you will change the world and also focus on what the community, the market, needs **and will support financially.** An entrepreneur, as opposed to a manager, will always think bigger. When a new project is discussed, whether it's a new organization or a new program, the entrepreneurial vision comes into play. The entrepreneur asks: how big an impact can this have? And the entrepreneur will be constantly aware of the political, social and economic contexts. For example, in light of an increasing number of unaccompanied minors from Central America coming to the county, Imagination Stage recognized a group of new children in the community who had yet to be served and developed programs to support their singular needs: Theatre for Change.

An entrepreneurial vision will be **BOLD!**

Before you start a nonprofit, ask yourself, and answer honestly, or as Jim Collins notes, brutally, in *Good to Great for the Social Sectors*: **is your vision for this new nonprofit venture truly something the community needs?** Or is your motivation to satisfy your own ego – or to provide an outlet for your own art? If this is **your motivation** you may find it hard to make the Case for Support when you look for board members, donors and others to support your *vision.*

In fact, the entrepreneur's nonprofit vision to meet the community need often results in creating the organization **first and following up with the requisite mission, vision and values statements.** The entrepreneur sees the need in the community, the opportunity that is unmet and **envisions** the future where the need is met and the world is better.

As noted in the introduction, this entrepreneurial perspective, meeting unmet needs in ways no one else is doing, is finding the Blue Ocean for the nonprofit business. Moreover, entrepreneurial nonprofits continue to see the Blue Oceans as they and their communities change over time. Imagination Stage offers an example of a 40-year business tradition of identifying the needs, seeing the opportunities and, regardless of risk, pursuing the solutions. One might say that Imagination Stage was a Blue Ocean company before the concept was even defined (Figure 1.1).

The Entrepreneurial Leader

No matter how compelling the vision, the organization may fail absent compelling leadership. Great entrepreneurial ideas often never leave the idea phase,

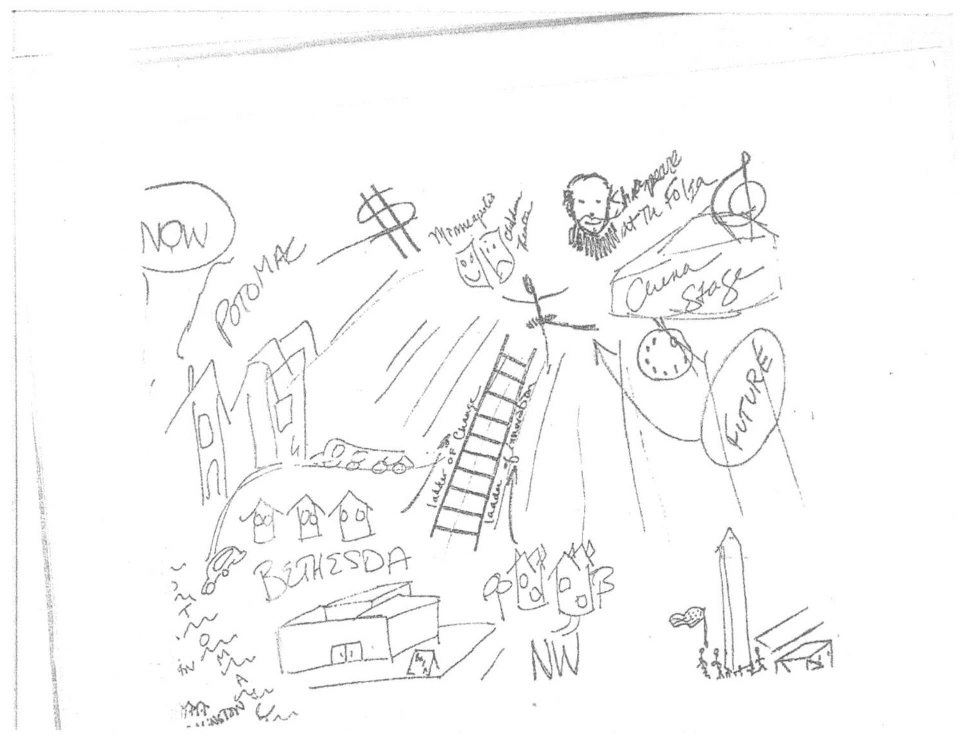

FIGURE 1.1: A visual representation of a planning session, sketch, 1990. We love this sketch because it illustrates that staff were always thinking entrepreneurially. We were a tiny organization but our artist imagined us as an important player in the DC arts landscape which IS what came to pass. Courtesy of Tim Reagan: BAPA Director of Education 1985–93.

never becoming more than jottings on a napkin unless the creator moves forward adopting the tenets of entrepreneurial leadership. One of the most frequently asked questions about leadership is: are great leaders born or made? We think the answer is a resounding yes! Some leaders are clearly born; others unexpectedly step up and "meet the moment." Research suggests that leaders are "mostly made."[15]

A commonly held belief is that great leaders are charming extroverts with engaging and empathetic personalities. This is often the case, but not always! Think about who *you* consider to be a great leader: a politician, a businessperson, a nonprofit administrator, where do they fall on the extrovert–introvert spectrum? There are many examples of great leaders who have engaging personalities (or who adopt them when necessary) but the reverse is often also true!

If you don't consider yourself charismatic and are concerned you won't be able to lead, this is good news – your leadership skills can be "developed."

Although we may not be born with the characteristics of leadership, we can learn them, emulate them and practice them. Remember the song from *The King and I:* "Whistle a Happy Tune"? It teaches that if you make yourself do something, even though you are not good at it, eventually you will perfect it. This is not to be confused with "fake it until you make it," i.e. lying about your abilities or your product. If you aspire to positions of leadership, then the best course is to embark on a leadership self-development plan. There are lots of opportunities for this, whether offered by organizations in person or online.

Begin practicing these traits of great entrepreneurial leaders:

- Get the best people involved,
- Practice humility: they do not consider themselves to be the smartest people in the organization,
- Practice emotional intelligence – the ability to understand social situations and processes is a critical component of leadership,
- Demonstrate ambition for the organization, not for yourself,
- Provide associates with opportunities for continued growth and success,
- Focus on delivering and sustaining great performance,
- Be disciplined, part of the team, not a show horse,
- Lead by example: leaders always do the right thing AND they move chairs and tables and shovel snow when necessary,
- Attribute success to others – or to good luck; attribute blame to yourself,
- Never stop learning: just as hairdressers continue to go to training sessions to learn new techniques, so business leaders ensure they continue to develop their leadership skills throughout their careers, attend seminars, workshops, etc.,
- Emulate Winston Churchill and never, never, never, never give up, and
- Demonstrate a sense of humor! When all else fails, this is especially essential.

Leadership of a visionary, entrepreneurial organization requires that those in charge create or maintain a compelling vision – one that stands the test of time. So, having a **Big Hairy Audacious Goal (BHAG)** (whether it is the vision/mission of the organization or a new business line) is a "must" for an organization. As developed in the book *Built to Last: Successful Habits of Visionary Companies* published in 1994 by Jim Collins and Jerry Porras,[16] and quoted by us endlessly. It's important to note that this book was not written for the nonprofit field. But that's fine. All nonprofits are also businesses, in the United States they are legally corporations. They have to engage in sound business practices to be successful. So, a book like this has much to offer both sectors and is one of our favorites along with Collins's *Good to Great* and *Good to Great for the Social Sector.*

At BAPA and at Imagination Stage, we have always been driven by this concept of **BHAGs**. BHAGs are informed by core values whose greatness is spelled out. It almost doesn't matter what the values are, only that they are compelling. Enduring great companies preserve their core values and purposes, while business strategies and operating practices endlessly adapt to a changing world. A true BHAG should: stimulate forward progress, create momentum, and excite associates and board members such that they throw their talents into it. For us, this became the driving framework for maintaining an entrepreneurial mindset every year. What was the BHAG for the year(s) that would move us closer to accomplishing our vision?

At BAPA/Imagination Stage, **our BHAG vision has always been that theatre must be a fundamental aspect of all children's lives.**

When we started our work, participation in theatre was not considered part of the fabric of a well-constructed life but a frill with no defining value. Indeed, some people even thought that a child might be seduced by arts involvement away from more practical past-times and careers. **And school systems did not then, and still do not, consider an arts education to be fundamental to a child's success.**

> *Combining a visionary and a manager is how you get things done. And Bonnie never lost her focus. The arts for all children was her mantra. The most effective, successful people learn from others, and, in turn become role models for others.*
>
> — Carol Trawick, entrepreneur, activist and philanthropist

Today, while the value of the arts is better understood and the arts are valued by more parents, the full power and potential of the arts have yet to be embraced.

The strength of the Imagination Stage vision holds firm. All children DO need the arts in their lives.

We believe that having audacious goals is essential to a flourishing nonprofit and that to move BHAGs forward, nonprofits must have entrepreneurial leaders who in addition to achieving superb results through unwavering resolve, must be humble, put the mission first and listen. This leads to a successful organization, which means they can answer with evidence:

- Are we successfully meeting our mission?
- Are we meeting financial goals?

With an entrepreneurial addition of:

- Can we do better?
- What more must we do?
- Can we serve more people with this project?

Throughout its 40+ years, Imagination Stage was successful in its impact and met its financial needs. The success of its programs in the community drove its growth. It did *not* grow for the sheer purpose of expansion. The vision and drive allowed Imagination Stage to adapt and grow to meet the needs of not only Montgomery County, Maryland but also the greater metropolitan area.

> *The first [secret to success] is courage because the world will constantly tell you what you cannot do and you have to have the courage to go for it. The second is confidence, if you have enough confidence you don't need a lot of courage. Third is competence. Nothing is better than knowing what you're doing. The fourth, which many people miss, is community.*
>
> — Reggie Van Lee, chair of the DC Arts Commission 2023 and a former partner at the Carlyle Group Prior; in an article by Peggy McGlone, Washington Post, November 28, 2011
>
> *When I think about Bonnie Fogel and leadership, I think about the requisites for success – purpose. She knew what she wanted from the start. She then came up with a plan. And a passion. And passion is what Bonnie really had a lot of. And then you need patience and perseverance and she had all of that.*
>
> — The Honorable Constance "Connie" Morella, former US congresswoman, former U.S. ambassador

In all businesses, especially entrepreneurial ones, there is a very fine line between what a leader KNOWS or can learn and an ability to make a decision based on experience, gut intuition and WISDOM.

> *Knowledge is knowing a tomato is a fruit;*
> *Wisdom is knowing not to put a tomato in a fruit salad.*
>
> — Eric Woiner, *The Socrates Effect*,[17] quoting Mike Kingsley

CASE STUDY: BAPA/IMAGINATION STAGE'S MULTIPLE ENTREPRENEURIAL EVOLUTIONS

As established above, nonprofits are created to meet a community's need. In 1979, Marcia Smith and I [Bonnie Fogel] were parents of children attending an elementary school in a suburb of Washington, DC. The need we saw was to provide local children with access to theatre performances and learning opportunities.

The enterprise began when a singular opportunity presented itself. The teachers in the school canceled the talent show because they didn't have time so we stepped in and produced it ourselves. Of the 340 children in the school, 300 wanted to be in it! We determined that everyone who wanted to be in the show should be. (This became the philosophy for the BAPA/Imagination Stage culture.) For those children with less developed artistic talent, we formed groups to whom we taught musical routines, dances, skits, acrobatics ... so that everyone, eventually, was part of the show. When the metaphorical curtain came down (we were in a school gym), we had an epiphany. We realized that we were not the only parents who wanted more creative opportunities for our children. The talent show was proof that children wanted it, and parents would support it. We wanted to provide that to the community. And, in that defining moment, our entrepreneurial spirits took over and we acted to answer a community need.

We created Bethesda Academy of Performing Arts (BAPA) which would eventually become Imagination Stage.[18] The immediate goal was to provide for our community, and the project resonated with other parents. As entrepreneurs, we accomplished the goal but then embraced the opportunity and kept growing. The enterprise grew out of a shared belief that there were very few opportunities for creativity in the local public schools and that this was detrimental to children's optimum growth and development. (See "Appendix A: The Origin Story" and "Appendix B: Chronology.")

We were busy over the summer incorporating the new nonprofit. The first classes were offered in September 1979 at a neighborhood elementary school that had closed due to declining demographics and was being used by the school system as an area office. The new enterprise was called Bethesda Academy of Performing Arts (BAPA), riffing off the famous British Royal Academy of Dramatic Arts (RADA). (Performing was substituted for Dramatic since BADA was not a great acronym!) Almost immediately, BAPA became the default name for the organization, so dubbed by its participants.

A MEETING OF THE MINDS

I grew up in New York City where exposure to the Arts, with a capital A, was in the air we breathed. Museums, concert halls, opera houses and stages were part of my childhood. I majored in dramatic arts at NYU and went on to act professionally and get my graduate degree in psychology.

When I had children, it became very important to me that they had the same exposure to the arts that I had. Arriving in Bethesda, I was surprised and disappointed to find that the funding for arts programs had been cut and the schools no longer offered children the opportunity for arts experiences.

I met Bonnie through a PTA program at Burning Tree Elementary School. We were kindred souls and after many cups of tea, BAPA was born.

Those first years were amazing. It was great fun, from constructing sets out of boxes, searching thrift stores for costumes and raiding our homes for set pieces, we produced plays. BAPA kids did Gilbert and Sullivan, formed a children's chorus and a competitive song and dance troupe. We even had a casting agency. It was a wonderful time, and I enjoyed every moment with the children and our small, dedicated staff. It definitely took "a village" to put BAPA on the map.

We did it all with no money, with a team of extraordinary, supportive parents and complete trust in each other.

— Marcia Smith, founder, executive director, Screen Actors Guild Foundation

I grew up in post-World War II England, everyone made their own music, put on their own entertainments, and had enormous fun doing so.

My young life was compromised: my mother, a single woman, provided for our bed and board as a housekeeper. We moved eleven times in my childhood which resulted in, among other things, my complete lack of an academic foundation. When I was 14, my luck changed when children's welfare authorities sent me to a boarding school to ensure continuity in my education.

The boarding school was attached to Lyme Regis Grammar School, a day school where the arts predominated. Here, for the first time, I was able to establish roots in an educational community and the arts provided a way for me to shine, despite my academic inadequacies. Drama, music, art provided a pathway for me to earn recognition, helped grow my self-confidence, and provided a joyful culture in which to grow. I wanted all this for my own children, and every other child who would benefit.

— Bonnie Fogel, founder

The immediate and ongoing success developed from our unshakeable belief in a vision and a passionate commitment to making that vision manifest. BAPA was always the embodiment of entrepreneurial leadership. The founders both had business backgrounds, understood the importance of building a business based on market needs and the importance of advertising and promoting to the best of their limited finances. In the next few years, the entrepreneurial spirit took hold, and many niche programs – unavailable elsewhere – were offered that ensured growing sales and interest in the start-up.

A defining moment for the fledgling organization occurred when Marcia left for California and a new life and career. Marcia had been the front woman and the artistic and educational talent; Bonnie was the administration. Members of the board stepped forward and said they wanted BAPA to continue and that Bonnie should do her best to keep it going. And she did. So this became not only a defining moment for our organization but was also the first **defining leadership moment.**

> *The world needs dreamers and the world needs doers. And, most especially, the world needs dreamers who do. Bonnie Fogel is a dreamer who did.*
>
> — The Honorable Christopher Van Hollen (Maryland's 8th Congressional District)

There were many **subsequent defining moments**, and the major ones reflect the **evolutions** of the small, scrappy community-based, nonprofit, into a world class, nationally recognized, **Theatre for Young Audiences** and education center serving 100,000+ annually. Each evolution started with a **defining moment**, a recognition of community need, challenges to overcome with grit and determination and entrepreneurial leadership.

Each evolution reflected an expansion of the mission – each evolution also represented a revisioning which reflected a changing community and world. **The foundational vision which imagined a world where theatre experiences are a fundamental aspect of children's lives remained constant.** And each evolution is built upon its own success to determine the next one.

1988 THE FIRST EVOLUTION: Expanding the Vision to Include Children with Access and Inclusion Needs. The theatre education classes were successful and enrollment was growing, as was the staff and board. And then we met an outstanding young educator, **Sally Dorothy Bailey**, who explained that children with physical and cognitive access and inclusion needs (then referred to as special needs) had an unmet yearning for creative outlets. BAPA invested precious resources in an **Arts Access Program** led by Ms. Bailey.

> *I also started the Pegasus performing company, for teens with and without disabilities. Each year we created original plays based on their ideas, so the play would be fit to their strengths and interests rather than the other way around. This allowed them to learn from each other, have an outlet for expressing their ideas, and explore new aspects of the world. I knew we were doing something right when at the end of each Pegasus season, the typically developing students announced, "I joined this group to help you [actors with disabilities], but instead you helped me." One performing company grew into two, then into three, and finally into four!*
>
> *So little was written about inclusive theatre at the time that I was given a summer to write Wings to Fly, a book about how to include everyone in theatre. The second edition, Barrier-Free Theatre, remains one of the few nuts and bolts handbooks in print about how to include everyone in the arts (available from Idyll Arbor, Inc.).*
>
> — Sally Dorothy Bailey, MFA, MSW, RDT/BCT director of arts access, 1989–99; professor, director of graduate studies in the theatre and director of the Drama Therapy Program, Kansas State University

Subsequently, a **Deaf Access Program** was launched, led by **Lisa Agogliati**, a BAPA dance teacher with an unrealized passion for bringing theatre arts to the Deaf community. Launching and maintaining these programs demanded a steadfast commitment. In the early days, some board members and parents, fearful of the unknown and concerned that programming would suffer for children who did not have access and inclusion needs, opposed the expansion. We were resolute, and four decades later Imagination Stage is a role model and access and inclusion is a philosophy not a program at that organization.

> *Lisa was a phenomenal teacher. When you are 16, you need that person in your life: young and fun, a mentor and a friend, the kind of person I needed and didn't have in other aspects of my life*
>
> — Joanne Seelig Lamparter, former Deaf Access company member and Imagination Stage Chief Artistic Programming Officer

Through the years, BAPA and Imagination Stage have received major recognition for this inclusion work and credit for starting programs that became national models. And, significantly, the success of these programs, which were informed by multiple intelligence theories, resulted in BAPA's adoption of a pedagogy for teaching that incorporated multiple intelligence practices. Furthermore, the inclusion work marked the beginning of the organization's commitment to **social justice theatre.**

1992: THE SECOND EVOLUTION: Expanding the Vision to Include Theatre for Young Audiences. BAPA teacher **Kathryn Chase Bryer** approached us with an idea: could she produce plays for young audiences using professional actors? From a business expansion viewpoint, there was an opportunity here – there were very few professional theatres offering Theatre for Young Audiences (TYA) in the region. And, we had the people who could make it successful. BAPA's Director of Education, **Janet Stanford** (who was to become Imagination Stage's Founding Artistic Director) was quick to agree and to step up to lead this new professional theatre. The immediate challenge was where to produce this new work. The organization's elementary school gym hosted student productions and putting a professional company there would be confusing to audiences. A new space was needed for this professional company. The vision to make a professional TYA theatre available and fundamental in children's lives opened a new potential market and created the next Blue Ocean opportunity.

I recalled a model I had seen in a Kansas City, MO, shopping center. Board President **Jerry Morenoff** and I set off to convince a nearby shopping center which was suffering from declining foot traffic, to let BAPA pilot a program in a closed store. No one in our region was making theatre for youth in a mall. But this was an untapped marketplace – offering theatre where the people were instead of making them come to a facility. A novel concept but one that was not an easy sell! But, again, having the right people on the bus – in this case the board president, an eminent businessman, made it happen. From the beginning the challenges were formidable: getting audiences to a new program in a new unconventional venue (whoever heard of a theatre in a shopping mall?), covering costs, maintaining the space and especially producing a quality theatre experience in a former woman's dress store with no stage, sound or lighting.

Within a couple of years, the investment had paid off. Shows were regularly sold out and productions achieved critical acclaim in *The Washington Post*. The work embodied our values with professional actors of all abilities. The success of this entrepreneurial venture led to the decision to look for a permanent home large enough to house a 400-seat theatre where Imagination Stage could, again, grow to meet the increasing demand for professional TYA.

> *From the moment I was introduced to BAPA/Imagination Stage, I experienced Carol Dweck's "growth mindset" at work. The leadership and mission were and are oriented to "what more can we do?," "how can we do it better" and "how can we serve more young people, especially those who are under-resourced."*
>
> — Sally Rosenberg, Esq., author, producer – Ladybug Productions, ninth board president, 2003–05

2003: THE THIRD EVOLUTION: Expanding the Vision to Include a Forever Home. The challenge to find a space large enough to house a 400-seat theatre plus classroom and office space was exacerbated when we learned that BAPA's educational space (a repurposed elementary school) was going to be razed to make room for a new high school. The pressure was intense as every conceivable location was investigated for a new, permanent home. In the end, an astute board member, **Gene Smith**, learned of an opportunity to build a nonprofit in a prospective county parking garage in downtown Bethesda, our nearest urban center. The challenge was to make the case that BAPA would be the best organization to meet the county's requirements. With inspiration from internationally renowned architect Ben Wood and the acumen of an increasingly sophisticated board and staff, a winning proposal was offered and accepted.

Whoever heard of a theatre in a parking garage? Whoever could dream of such a thing? Probably the same people who had dreamed and produced a theatre in a shopping mall! Entrepreneurial visionaries. That's who.

So, Imagination Stage partnered with the county government to establish a permanent home in a county garage in the heart of downtown Bethesda, Maryland. And now the real challenge began, a nonprofit that had previously raised only $250,000 for annual support, needed to raise $13M to cover construction, licensing, and furnishing, fixtures and equipment costs. All but the final $4M was raised which was covered by a bank loan and eventually paid off by Carol and Jim Trawick, local philanthropists with a passion for local children's causes.

> *In the beginning, we talked about wouldn't it be great if we had our own physical structure? Wouldn't it be great if we had our own theatre? And, maybe we could change our name so that it wasn't just connected to Bethesda, but to a larger organization. And every time we talked about it; it seemed like that was really impossible And we would laugh about it. But you know what, it happened.*
>
> — Barbara "Bobbie" J. Gottschalk, BAPA/Imagination Stage, second president and co-founder, Seeds of Peace

In this new 42,000 sq. ft. home, the business was reinvented including a name change, **Imagination Stage**, which reflected the company's growing emphasis on professional theatre. The new home established what was to become a nationally recognized **Theatre for Young Audiences** and the rapid expansion of all aspects of the business. The move, which was a very big lift for a modest still-scrappy organization, resulted in explosive growth of 500 percent and won the company the distinction of being named by ***Inc.*** magazine as one of the nation's fastest-growing private companies. In the early days, the challenges were endless, and mainly financial as income had to be ratcheted up significantly to cover the huge increase in expenses. But the vision was made manifest by this Forever Home (Figure 1.2).

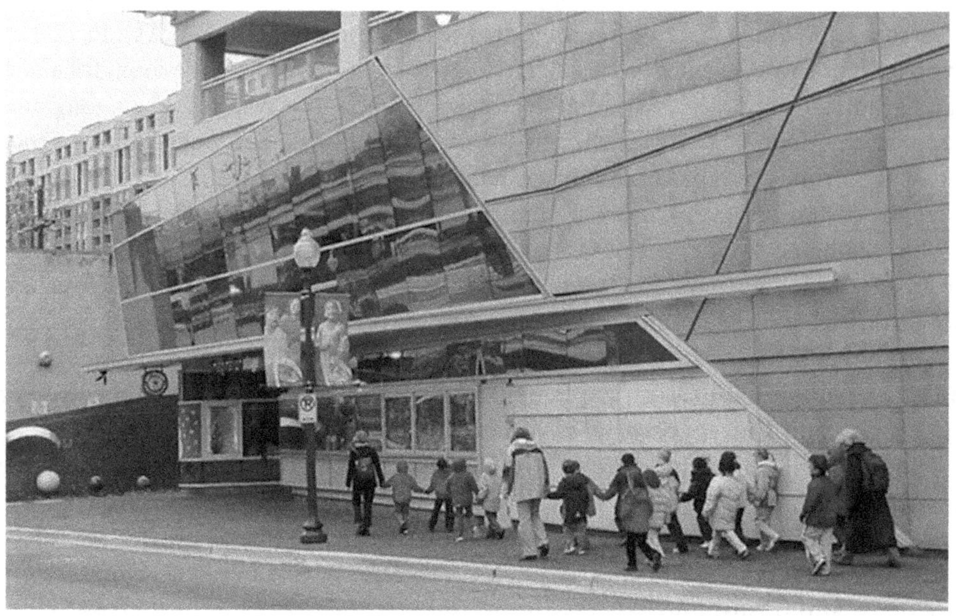

FIGURE 1.2: Imagination Stage's Forever Home, located inside a public parking garage in partnership with Montgomery County, Maryland, 2003. Photo courtesy of Imagination Stage.

> *You often come across people with visionary thoughts, but the ability to actually be able to turn that into action and execute a plan and turn it into something like Imagination Stage is truly remarkable. Vision. Imagination. Perseverance. This has been evident in the development of BAPA and Imagination Stage.*
>
> — The Honorable Gabe Albornoz, council member, Montgomery County, Maryland

2014: THE FOURTH EVOLUTION: Expanding the Vision to Washington, DC. the success of Imagination Stage led to the consideration of expansion. DC was the logical place to do so. Imagination Stage DC was launched to respond to the lack of professional **Theatre for Young Audiences** and theatre education in the District of Columbia. At the same time, social justice theatre and theatre education enjoyed a defining moment when Artistic Director **Janet Stanford** heard a radio broadcast about the unaccompanied minors from Central America who were arriving in our community. The opportunity to serve another marginalized community was evident and she rightly construed that trauma-informed drama activities could help. The formula of county agencies working with Imagination Stage educators and artists was replicable in other areas. This led to the establishment of the

Theatre for Change program and subsequent work with displaced children, police/community relations, and incarcerated youth. (Indeed, in some ways we see this work as the fifth evolution.) This work has also presented a new opportunity not only to expand programming to meet new markets but also to find new sources of government grants and philanthropic support. Again, a steady commitment to the expansion by staff and board was imperative to overcome all the hurdles of a new organization in DC and, concomitantly, the launch of the new Theatre for Change programming operation. Again, this vision expanded to serve a new population with theatre experiences.

> *It reminded me of the work I had done decades ago about women who had suffered from domestic violence. I learned then that people who have been through terrible trauma can go from feeling like victims to feeling like survivors, which is a huge empowering discovery for them. The process works the same way for any kid who has been through trauma and devastating grief.*
>
> – Janet Stanford, artistic director, 1993–2024

The four evolutions that were pivotal to Imagination Stage's development would not have happened, and the expansion of the organization would not have occurred absent an ongoing commitment to seizing entrepreneurial opportunities that met emerging community needs. Continually ensuring vision and mission alignment with the current and future work allowed the organization to marshal the strengths of the appropriate people to get the job done and steadfastly overcome the challenges that all new ventures face.

Sometimes new ideas were not sustainable and did not lead to an evolutionary shift in the organization. Sometimes because we were "ahead of the curve" but sometimes because we did not have the right staff leadership or board support to make them happen at the time.

From the beginning and through four decades, the vision/mission and entrepreneurial practice of first BAPA and then Imagination Stage was tightly tied to **meeting community needs and engaging new markets.** Whether it was for theatre arts education, opportunities for children with access and inclusion needs, professional theatre productions, expansion to communities not served or prioritization of social justice issues – the essence of **the entrepreneurial spirit of its leadership**.

Importantly, each evolution provided the bedrock to achieve the next. For instance, a new arts educational pedagogy informed by understanding how to work with young people with inclusion needs led to a commitment to help other marginalized communities. **Entrepreneurialism at its root is about seeing and meeting a need**

***and* seeing new sources of business.** At Imagination Stage new programs serving new populations also led to new sources of earned and contributed income.

VISION + OPPORTUNITY = SUCCESS (MEETING MISSION AND FINANCIAL GOALS)

Despite the expanded programming, the founding vision and mission have only been tweaked through the years, not changed. The basic *raison d'etre* of Imagination Stage remains true to its original vision: that all children need the arts in their lives. This upholding of a basic motivating belief is essential for an authentic and successful business whether for profit or nonprofit.

Through the years, as the organization has grown in sophistication and understanding and, as the community has changed, so too has the manifestation of that vision into the company's mission and practice, both have developed, have expanded and contracted, to meet community needs. But, at its center the vision and core belief has always been simple. All children need the arts in their lives.

All children means:

- regardless of their economic circumstances, and/or
- the speed of their cognition or the strength of their limbs, and/or
- their cultural heritage, and/or
- their gender identity, and/or
- their (or their parents') dreams for their future.

This is a culture that always responds to the "needs of now."

— Janet Stanford, founding artistic director, 1993–2024

Critical to success in achieving our vision was recognizing that the circumstances of our community change across time – and as nonprofit entrepreneurs we must always be ready to meet the newest challenge or opportunity.

The Wrap

Entrepreneurial traits we identified and focused on in this chapter were:

- Visionary – they identify opportunities in the nonprofit's community;
- Market savvy – they can "read" the market to determine if this will sell.

Entrepreneurial leaders are visionary – they see a need and have a vision of how to provide the solution and they take action. They, unlike traditional managers, are able to link the need to the solution and make their vision manifest. Organizations with an entrepreneurial mindset repeat the process continually. They see emerging needs, make solutions and the company evolves over time. Maintaining entrepreneurship over time requires always scanning the environment in order to identify and meet the next need. Entrepreneurial leaders read broadly, from local news to emerging business model texts to enduring literature. It is, in fact, a core entrepreneurial business practice. Nonprofits, truly any business, that do not evolve to meet changing community needs will go out of business.

Entrepreneurial visionaries who succeed are also entrepreneurial leaders who identify core values aligned with a BHAG. Pursuing a BHAG is part of pursuing a lofty, meaningful vision that changes the world. But, the key to success is measuring what matters. Missions assume an impact and resultant change. Missions are made manifest by focused programs. By creating strong program evaluation pathways in your organization, you will be able to prove that your work has the desired impact.

Discussion Questions For Starting Or Growing Entrepreneurial Leaders

- Starters:
  - Are you a born leader, or are you going to make yourself into a leader? How will you approach this task?
  - Under what circumstances might a vision or mission statement be changed?
  - Consider your local news and conversations, what are the needs facing your community? Write a vision and mission statement to articulate how you might address meeting them.
- Adaptors:
  - Review your mission and vision, do they meet the expectations articulated in the chapter?
- How can your organization engage in mission-focused work to meet those needs?
  - Is this a Blue or Red Ocean?
  - Are you doing more of the same thing or will this idea grow new markets?
- What are there untapped opportunities or markets that you talk about?
  - What would it take to make it happen (broadly speaking)?

Trait 2

It's All about the People: Staff and Board

Get the Right People on the Bus ...

—Jim Collins

Surround yourself only with people who are going to take you higher.

—Oprah Winfrey

In any business enterprise, regardless of how innovative and extraordinary your leader's vision and how much the nonprofit program is needed, the first and most important priority is that a leader be surrounded by professional associates and board members with the skills and resources to make that vision happen.

There are shelves upon shelves of best practices for human resources. *Entrepreneurial Arts and Cultural Leadership* does not attempt to add to that literature. We do recommend that you hire a human resource specialist to support the practices described below. This is not a traditional priority in nonprofits, but the entrepreneurial mindset, which values human resources above all, makes it one. In this chapter, we spotlight this previously identified entrepreneurial trait:

- People – Entrepreneurs engage the right people to help them.

While Imagination Stage always had an individual tasked with human resource development, once we grew into our Forever Home, and our staff associates increased significantly, we believed that if we were to uphold our stated core values, a Director of Human Resources became a necessity. If we were to uphold our values codes and statements, we had to employ someone who would ensure that associates felt valued, that the organization was abiding by all the changing laws as well as offering structures and supports for associates including coordinating reviews to managing staff health clinics.

While abiding by best practices in human resources is essential, understanding your core purpose of hiring associates is critical. For many that is hiring someone to accomplish a task. For Imagination Stage and most socially focused enterprises, that isn't enough. For us, the key was always finding the right people. The expression "getting the right people on the bus" was coined by Jim Collins in his 2001 publication *Good to Great: Why Some Companies Make the Leap ... and Others Don't*. Every student of best management practices (for profit or nonprofit) should read it. Collin's idea is not new, it's a sensible approach to leadership excellence, but his bus imagery stuck and we used it as a catchphrase at Imagination Stage.

Collins's book analyzes what makes a great company. When they were researching the book, they expected to find that the formula for success would be (1) vision, (2) strategy for accomplishment and (3) getting people aligned behind it. Instead, they found that **great leaders start with "who" rather than "what."** They know that if you have the right people, they will be able to adapt to an always-changing world. Conversely, if you have the wrong people, they can and will drag the company down. This is true for all companies regardless of tax status.

Entrepreneurial leaders make the vision manifest. **So, the first step when starting a new business, or re-starting an existing one, is to get the right people on the bus, people who complement their leader's skills.** The "right people" are those who share the leader's passion for the vision, while also being confident self-starters. At arts and cultural organizations, they likely have social intelligence and socio-emotional skills and are people who the leader can trust to uphold their values, programs and organizational culture.

Getting the right people working in your organization is the first step; the next steps are critical to keeping them there:

- Listen to them: **listen with curiosity, rather than waiting to insert your own opinions.** Think about it. Most people in conversation are merely waiting to insert their own knowledge, rather than truly listening to what is being said, responding to it with deep inquiry and an openness to new ideas. Good leaders engage in **dialogue and discussion.**
- Empower them. The right people are self-motivated. If you empower them, they don't need extraneous team-building exercises. One way to *de*motivate people is to ignore them, ignore facts and not listen.
- Honor them. At every opportunity show them you care, informally or publicly.

> *In South Africa, there is a Zulu greeting, "Sawubona." It means hello, but when translated literally it means "I see you." When leaders use it, they mean: "I recognize that what you feel is real." The customary reply to Sawubona is Yebo Sawubona, which means "I see you seeing me." It implies "when you recognize me in all my full humanity, I recognize you too, and I honor your acknowledgement of me."*
>
> — Jen Fisher and Anh Nguyen Phillips[19]

Equally importantly, the entrepreneurial leader will **get the wrong people off the bus.** So many organizations keep poorly performing associates on because:

- "They have been here for a long time and know the organization," and/or
- "They are really good at their job and will be impossible to replace," and/or
- "The devil you know is better than the devil you don't know," and/or
- "They would cost too much to replace," and/or
- "Management doesn't have the time" or energy to conduct a search for a new associate.

The damage of having the wrong people or the disengaged is significant. When you don't remove badly performing associates, they can poison the culture through snide comments about the mission, leadership or their peers. They can prevent work from moving forward by adopting an entrenched position. They can fight and slow down the needed change or innovation in the organization. The situation is almost always complex. Thus, before moving forward on the process, a true entrepreneurial leader seeks counsel with their lawyers, human resources or union representatives depending on the situation.

In every case, at Imagination Stage, when a poor associate was eventually replaced, the new hire was superior and the culture of the organization improved dramatically almost immediately.

Let's imagine: your vision is clear and you've hired all the right people. Essentially, continuing the metaphor, the bus is loaded with terrific associates and it's hurtling along the highway that is a developing business' journey, doing excellent work and building up speed and energy at every turn. Now it's time to retain employees by keeping them motivated, supported and engaged.

Many of even the best corporations focus on hiring and forget about onboarding, training or continuing education and support.

- **Onboarding:** No one comes into an organization ready to start at full speed. Even if they did the same job somewhere else, your company has a different culture, different policies and protocols and likely different software. Taking the time to onboard is critical. At Imagination Stage, all new hires had an in-person meeting with the founder and the artistic director to learn the history and the culture; we called it Imagination Stage 101. And, we created a first meeting form that helped the HR director with the managing director identify what training was necessary. For example, many apprentices didn't know how to use Microsoft Excel at the expected level. And, employees using more advanced and customized donor or audience software almost always benefit from at least a refresher course from the vendor. Onboarding should also include corporate procedures and norms, introducing the employee to the strategic plan, developing their work plan and supervision norms and explaining how to do the basics – from copying to requesting vacation time.

- **Professional development** offers many staff members an opportunity to learn more about their work and how to do it better. Investing in expanding and supporting employees not only increases their skills, knowledge and engagement with their work but also increases the knowledge within the organization as they share and model what they learned.
- **Active supervision** and support are critical to retaining the best and the brightest. Many HR specialists recommend a short, five-minute check-in weekly and a more formal monthly conversation as well as the annual review. This prevents frustration from developing from unanswered questions and provides a frequent venue for the employee to communicate their wants and needs for success to their supervisor.

Overall, getting and keeping the right people involves recognizing that success for the individual employee is success for the organization. As is evident from above and in the following case study, entrepreneurs exceed best practices and engage with the right people to meet an expanding vision and opportunity.

CASE STUDY: IMAGINATION STAGE'S PEOPLE MAKE IT HAPPEN

Part of entrepreneurial leadership is recognizing that finding the right people is a critical step in achieving your vision. Much like in a theatre production, a director's job is 80 percent casting the right actors. And, like directing, it doesn't always work out right, but when it does, the people stick, and their work amplifies the mission and impact of the organization. This also requires making retention a priority. At Imagination Stage, it speaks volumes that the artistic director and associate artistic directors have both been at the organization for over 30 years. Kate Bryer joined in 1989 and Janet Stanford in 1993. Many, if not most, key employees stay well over the national average of 3.5 years.[20] And, with a stable leadership and growing organization, new voices and perspectives are always sought as opportunities arise.

Retention must be a priority. It's not always possible to do this; superior employees are always going to find new opportunities. Recognizing this, at Imagination Stage, we ensured that we made the most of all associates for as long as we had them. The key is understanding that **retention** starts at the top. And that it is **personal** from the leadership and requires **strategic commitment**.

For instance, we engaged in new rituals and practices to show our appreciation for associates. Unlike many organizations, we always held a party to celebrate their work with the company. And, one of the most appreciated by associates was the Golden Boomerang, a cheap child's toy I spray-coated gold. The practice had two intentions: (1) to encourage them to return at some point (and several did); (2) to show the remaining staff how much they were valued.

When we finally moved into our Forever Home, we inscribed the names of current staff associates onto the walls. We felt they were just as important as the donors whose names were on the donor walls.

> *Of course I was thrilled and honored to receive the Golden Boomerang; it was a gift of thanks, trust and camaraderie. My years at BAPA and Imagination Stage were personally and professionally fulfilling. The staff Bonnie assembled was so talented in so many complementary ways that our big dreams couldn't help but be realized. The passion behind the mission was almost exclusively due to leadership's dedication to, and belief in, every member of the staff. The trust that was placed in us was humbling and staggering. To those of us who received the boomerang, it was a symbol of that trust. It was so inspiring and heartwarming to know that our talents would always be welcomed at Imagination Stage.*
>
> — Richard Bradbury, Imagination Stage producing artistic director for the Studio Theatre, 1997–2006; Olivet Boys and Girls Club, Center for the Arts, Reading, PA

Entrepreneurial leaders recognize everyone wants to feel valued. The entrepreneurial leader is aware of the value of *all* employees, and clearly states, at every opportunity, their understanding of the value of each and every employee. At Imagination Stage, we attended, when possible, after-work drinks parties, afternoon runs for ice cream, sending birthday greetings and meeting in-person one-on-one with not only those we supervised but as many employees as possible. When an executive models this behavior to their leadership team, there is a good chance that leadership team members will then adopt this practice with their own teams. These moments serve as listening tours, hearing what your employees value and want and finding ways to meet their needs. For example, during the Great Recession, we started a listening circle for our younger employees who felt they had ideas that weren't being heard. One of the many new practices we adopted was a new birthday party model that emphasized group sales for productions over the traditional birthday party model.

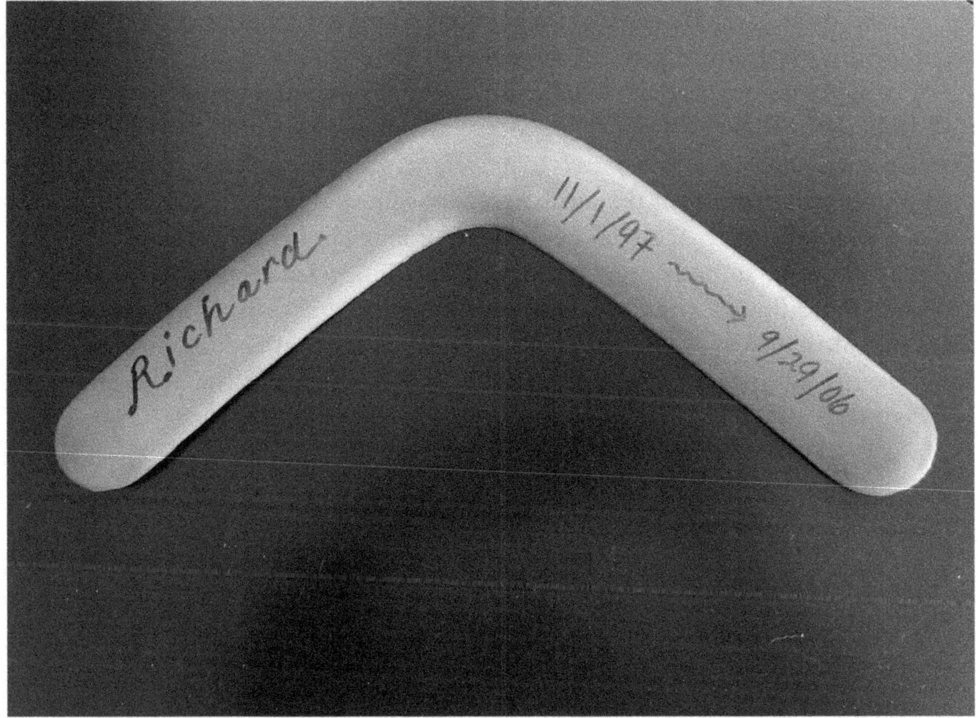

FIGURE 2.1: The Richard Bradbury boomerang, 2006. Photo courtesy of Richard Bradbury.

By listening and valuing all employees, the culture of the organization solidifies, making it easier to attract, maintain and advance excellent employees.

> *The major contributing factor to the 40+ years of success for Imagination Stage has been the commitment of those who work there to the inclusion and success of each child who walks through the doors.*
>
> — David Markey, deputy director, commission on the arts and humanities, Government of the District of Columbia; Imagination Stage director of education (2001–13)

Empowering your staff is critical. You would think that leaders would have a solid understanding of how to do this. But that is not always the case. Oftentimes, hours are spent on motivational team-building exercises that really wouldn't be needed if staff were properly valued and empowered in the first place. For example, staff need to feel connected to the mission and value such that they have a place to grow. There should be examples of people who have advanced their careers within the organization. And they need to know that no matter what position they were hired for there is a future here for them.

At Imagination Stage, there were many examples of junior employees who rose to lead departments. And not in the departments they started in. For example, **Lisa Agogliati** started as a dance instructor and grew in the company becoming the founder and director of the Deaf Access program. **Patricia Kratzer** began as a teacher and went on to become the director of finance. **Lynn Mattingly** began as a volunteer and eventually grew to be the director of education. This is often not practiced in traditional organizations where leaders look outside to bring in new ideas and talent which leads to the disillusionment of those already on staff and their subsequently leaving the organization because their ideas and voices go unheard.

> Leadership should always be about cheerleading – especially staff associates. A fine example of this can be found at Imagination Stage where the walls are emblazoned with quotes. When we came into the building, the idea was to manifest our beliefs on the importance of our mission on our walls. Staff determined which of about 100 quotes should be used, ensuring that arts disciplines and quotes about children would be prioritized.
>
> Greeting staff at the top of the stairs leading to the staff quarters is this wonderful quote from Founding Artistic Director Janet Stanford:
>
> *To open a heart, inspire a thought,*
> *ignite an imagination:*
> *That's why we came to work today.*

Additionally, supporting associates' interests in the organization beyond their assigned roles can offer life-changing opportunities for them. **Wendy Hamilton** worked in fundraising but had a passion for professional theatre and for supporting children of all abilities. Her passions led her to volunteer and support the Arts Access program, engaging in work that helped the students and the organization while impacting her life at a deeply personal level.

> *I had always dreamed of working for a professional children's theatre that also offered classes and performance opportunities for youth of all abilities. And, when I discovered Imagination Stage, it seemed to be too good to be true! Not only was I exposed to some of the best arts management practices in the country, but also I was encouraged to participate in Wings! the AccessAbility theatre troupe for adults with mixed abilities. My experiences in the group's therapeutic theatre exercises led to a life-changing autism diagnosis in my own family.*
>
> — Wendy Hamilton, associate director of institutional development, 2002–07, Major Gifts Officer, Planned Parenthood

Entrepreneurial leadership understands the strengths of people on their team. Years ago, Imagination Stage administered the **Torrance Test for Creativity** to all board and staff members. The exercise was designed to show how creativity CAN be identified, evaluated, taught and learned. Leadership was very surprised to discover that **they** were not the most creative people on staff! Indeed, the associates who graded highest were two of the most junior members. From then on, those two members were invited to all the meetings when leadership was considering a new program or direction.

How can an organization ensure the same degree of **commitment** at every level of the organization? The key is making sure that every member of the staff understands how they are contributing to the mission and impact of the work. There's a wonderful story about **President John F. Kennedy's** visit to the NASA Space Station very early on in the space program's infancy when manned space travel was still a dream. During his walk-about, he stopped to talk to a floor sweeper, introduced himself and then asked the employee what his job at NASA was. The employee said: "I am working to get a man on the moon." That is an example of staff empowerment at its finest. Every employee at NASA knew the company's ultimate mission and how they were instrumental to its success.

As a nonprofit dedicated to education, Imagination Stage began an apprenticeship program (full time with salary and benefits) for early career theatre managers. These individuals became the fuel and energy of the organization, and in return, we offered them a view of the world of nonprofit business. Everyone worked with the apprentices, and we all learned from one another.

> *I was in the first class of apprentices. I still talk to people about the educational experience of working in every department, learning how different departments work and work together. It was an incredible experience and program.*
>
> — Christina Rutter, board relations manager, San Francisco Symphony, Imagination Stage: 2003–07: volunteer coordinator, apprentice, marketing associate

Ensuring the same level of commitment to the mission from associates requires the following:

- It starts with **communications** from the top. Leadership must consistently address the mission. Branding that reflects the distinctive style, products and culture of the organization helps associates understand the organization they work for. Even the building's design and décor can speak to the mission and practice of the organization, again, in such a way that reaches employees on a subliminal level, they live and breathe organizational culture which strengthens their commitment and sense of belonging.

- Thoughtful **planning**, tied to mission and awareness of changing business and cultural landscapes, is not only essential for organizational growth but also its strategic execution and communication **builds employee loyalty and retention.** Excellent planning starts with a comprehensive and metrics-driven **Strategic Plan.** At Imagination Stage, we advise a three-year plan that is regularly updated. These plans are then built out and communicated through individual work plans for each staff member.

For many organizations, the value of the **Strategic Plan** takes place when it is being written, when team planning members are laser-focused on the opportunities and threats facing the organizations. At Imagination Stage, unlike standard organizations, all staff were engaged in development at various points during the process of creating the strategic plan to ensure their commitment and understanding of the organization's larger, institutional goals.

Ensuring that comprehensive work on strategic planning is not lost but becomes part of the organization's ongoing practice also supports **team building.** At Imagination Stage, we made the strategic plan a core component of everyone's work. Entrepreneurial leaders ensure that "just getting the job done" isn't enough – why the job is being done has to be transparent and reinforced. This process took time, intention and focus but resulted in success.

Well ahead of the beginning of each new fiscal year, we presented goals for the upcoming year that identify aspects of the **Strategic Plan** that were to be completed and budgeted. At Imagination Stage, we created **Best Practice** in a one-sheet **Annual Dashboard (see Appendix G)** that uses metrics and narrative to identify annual goals and the point person responsible for fulfillment.

Following leadership board and staff approval, the Dashboard then informed the annual budget and each **Department's Work Plans** for the year. Again, the department's work plan was based on the Dashboard which is tied to the **Strategic Plan.** Most importantly, each and every member of the **staff was then provided with their own personal plan of work** against which their work was reviewed throughout the year and used as a tool for evaluating them in their annual review. Each associate understood that their work was tied to the annual budget and goals, which in turn were tied to the three-year **Strategic Plan.** They then knew how their own personal effort connected to meeting the organization's mission – **whether it is putting a man on the moon, or feeding a hungry child or bringing theatre to the community.**

Transparent organizational structure: the metaphor for the well-run, open, organizational practice can be likened to a fishbowl: "nothing to see here." In small organizations, everyone knows everyone's business. In the early 1980s, BAPA secured a very small office space in the elementary school in which it rented space for its classes. The space had been the kitchen for the school – so it came equipped with a sink! We were in heaven. We managed to squeeze three desks into the 100 sq. ft. space – and two extra chairs for visitors. I told the team of four part-time staff: "we don't need to have meetings to know what is going on, just listen in on everyone's phone calls!"

> *I loved the close-knit community. I loved the compelling mission and being part of a team that was doing something extraordinary. Unlike the Joni Mitchell song about tearing down paradise to build a parking lot, we were building paradise inside a parking garage.*
>
> — Judi Canter, director capital campaign, 1999–2004

That culture of transparency remained, even when the organization grew. In the same way that the founding mission and vision for the organization never changed, so the DNA of Imagination Stage always reflected an open, caring, empowered culture. If you visited, the vibe reminded you of an old-time newspaper office: everyone's desks abutting, no private offices and a terrific energy and buzz resulting from phone calls and conversations that were, literally, out in the open. As Judi Canter explained, "When I think about Imagination Stage, I think about loyalty and trust. It is in the DNA of the organization."

It's a style that works. Thirty years later, "open planning" in office spaces was the way to go. The energy that emanated from this kind of workspace ensured teamwork and a constant hum of excitement, accomplishment and connection. And it's the way the Forever Home for Imagination Stage was designed. To ensure the energy wasn't locked away behind doors, the "water cooler" moments were happening even at your desk.

As a staff grows larger, it is harder to maintain transparency. Some conversations DO need to take place behind a closed door. Some meetings must accommodate thoughtful conversation without distraction. That said, in almost every case, notes from those meetings can be widely shared. Every staff member cannot (and should not) attend every meeting, but access to the discussions can be available and shared.

As Imagination Stage grew from two part-time employees to a full-time equivalent staff of over 50, leadership worked to maintain a flat culture aiming for staff empowerment and transparency.

> *Control has never been a thing at Imagination Stage, we've never felt threatened by other people's ideas. When I am a director, I feel like a collaborator and a facilitator.*
>
> — Kate Bryer, director of theatre, 1989–present

In arts management parlance, although we didn't realize it at the time, we were modeling a light version of **holacracy**: a system that distributes authority and decision-making through self-organizing teams ensuring a greater degree of transparency, effectiveness and agility. The term was **coined by Brian Robertson in 2007.**[21] Holacracy aims to provide a sense of purpose at every level: organizational purpose, team purpose and individual purpose are all explicit and aligned. And, holacracy empowers everyone to act as a sensor for the organization. It provides clear pathways to turn challenges into opportunities for improvement.

At its most realized, a holacracy is a system for managing a company where there are no assigned roles and employees have the flexibility to take on various tasks and move between teams freely. The organizational structure is flat, with little hierarchy. This is in direct opposition to the hierarchical norm of corporations, nonprofit or otherwise.

We naturally evolved in that direction as we sought to empower associates through this flatter structure. Some examples of our holacracy-light practice include:

- Instead of sequestering social media to a single person or department, all staff were encouraged to **post on social media** about Imagination Stage.
- Notes from Imagination Stage leadership team's weekly meetings were **shared with all members of staff.**
- Staff were empowered through staff-run committees to **bring issues to management.**
- **A weekly one sheet** detailing the highs and lows in each department was distributed by executive leadership to all staff and board members ensuring **transparency** and equal opportunity to share department news.
- An **Institutional Development** department streamlines and aligns communications from marketing and development departments to prevent internal competition while vying for attention from patrons, parents and audience members. The departments worked together to:
  - devise shared campaigns around current productions or special events, and
  - schedule all audience contacts via a comprehensive matrix that tracks the interior and exterior work of all departments.

This organizational "de-siloization" made the work entirely transparent, saved time and energy, avoided territorial disputes and ensured audiences, patrons and donors weren't inundated with information. By empowering the entire company, the entrepreneurial vision became an organizational mindset.

When growing an organization, entrepreneurial leaders need to ensure that the company is adaptive, nimble and open-minded, in business practice AND in organizational practice. They need to have the right people on the bus, at the right time, doing the right thing, together.

HOW ENTREPRENEURIAL LEADERSHIP BUILDS A STAFF TEAM OF ASSOCIATES

Getting **any** staff on the bus is the biggest challenge to any leader. Regardless of where you are on your organization's growth chart, finding staff is always the biggest hurdle. This is mission-centric.

- Focus on **finding people** who are excited by your vision and mission. If you are a nonprofit doing work that is important, there will always be people who want to join you.
- **Hiring people** is difficult for a nonprofit with a limited budget. Regardless of whether you are starting an organization or an institution, meeting salary expectations can be really tough. Over the years, Imagination Stage struggled mightily to make our original inadequate salary structure work for the people we really wanted to engage. Creative solutions were invoked. For instance:

  - We offered a four-day week *in lieu* of the salary that we could not meet and were successful. And our hire was so productive in those four days that we didn't regret it.
  - We covered 100 percent health insurance and prioritized travel and parking subsidies.
  - We approached someone who was well out of our league financially, but, in conversation, it turned out that a job closer to home and a passion for our work sealed the deal.

While you need to have passion inside day-to-day operations, having people on your board who have expertise and training outside your nonprofit's work can be valuable. Use every opportunity to network, and not just within your industry. Imagination Stage's membership with the local Chamber of Commerce proved tremendously beneficial in terms of board prospects, donors, sales and new associates.

Lastly, **grow your own.** Obviously, you must play the long game here … but an apprenticeship program, which has all kinds of benefits at the moment, also is a training ground for prospective employees. By the time they join the staff, they have the culture in their DNA and know what to expect from their full-time payroll position. At Imagination Stage, we started an apprenticeship program that lasted nine months. It then became a year. We then added a journeyman position to extend an exceptional apprentice an additional year to keep their energy and knowledge in the fold. At Imagination Stage, a former student now leads our education department. Talk about **growing our own!**

> *I remember Bonnie saying to me: "you're doing so many things, you are spreading yourself too thin. Talk to me about what the one thing is you'd really like to do, and let's see if we can make it work for you here." I said that I really wanted to direct a team of professional actors in plays. I felt we could do professional theatre for children in a sustained basis. It happened and it was good for me, and it was good for the organization.*
>
> — Kate Bryer, director of theatre, 1989–present

ADDITIONAL STAFF RESOURCES

As nonprofit leaders, we can't all be endowed with the talents of the entrepreneurial geniuses of our day. Still, we **can** maximize our business acumen by surrounding ourselves with the savviest most market-aware people in our community. After hiring the best marketing and promotions team you can, look to the community and entice its most successful members to join your board.

Board members are part of the team. Engaging them as a true team member is an entrepreneurial attribute. Again, according to where you are on your organization's journey, you may *need* to make more or less use of your board members to support or expand staff responsibilities. But, even at some quite established nonprofits, board members can be intricately involved in day-to-day work, simply by sending marketing posts on their social media or significantly by stepping in to be interim directors or CFOs. Although this is not recommended on a standing basis, it can really help in a crisis. And some organizations with very scant resources use their board members to run the organization.

> *In 2010 I received a call from Bonnie whom I had never met. She had heard of me and my Bethesda real estate business. She asked if I would agree to meet with her to discuss an idea she had. She was sizing me up to see if I would make a good board member. Unaware of her true intentions, I listened to her project idea and agreed to contribute my time and energy to make it happen. That is how Bonnie built her amazingly productive boards over the years. She never stopped searching for the next talented or connected person to approach and get to know.*
>
> — Jane Fairweather, realtor, The Jane Fairweather Team, former chair, Bethesda/Chevy Chase Chamber of Commerce, Imagination Stage board president, 2013–15; Imagination Stage DC board president, 2013–14

We recommend nurturing a culture that embraces **partnerships and consultants (see Trait 4). Partnerships** can be especially helpful when it comes to needing additional staff to expand a program into a new business area or community. Sometimes, mission can be met more effectively by partnering with a nonprofit that shares your mission and is already in that space. Mutual benefits can arise that go well beyond getting the work done. Donors and elected officials love to hear about partnerships, especially when new work is accomplished that improves the community. And partners help us see beyond our sometimes narrow view point and bring new energy to our organizations.

Consultants are also turned to for stop-gap help when finding the right person for the bus is taking too long. But hiring a consultant should be considered carefully, as they can be a considerable drain on financial and staff resources. They can be a resource but are not advised as a standing solution to a staffing problem because usually the consultant does not have your culture in their DNA and hangs up their hat when they walk out of the door. We often hired consultants for web design or one-time projects. Some, however, ended up coming back again and again, becoming part of the team as an external support. For example, **Cynthia Friedman** became our core graphic designer as an independent contractor. She began with us for one project and then became the lead for our core visual products (season brochures, gala invitations and class brochures).

> *The world is littered with failed arts organizations created as the extensions of egos of founders. Imagination Stage was not an extension of Bonnie's ego. She invited people to come in with their own ideas. She had a knack for talking to everybody: to a funder, to government officials, to parents, to children, to playwrights, to actors. She wasn't limited in her worldview and her perspective. And she brought those people in to join her. And that was one of the great strengths that she brought to Imagination Stage. The foundation that she laid and the organization that she created, the staff that she built, will linger long after she's gone.*
>
> — Frank Allen Philpot, Imagination Stage founding president, former PBS Kids executive, assistant professor of marketing, George Mason University, VA
>
> *I've always respected people that find people who know more than they do. You can always hire someone that isn't as good as you, Bonnie hired people who knew more than she did and people she thought were better than her. And that's something to admire. And she also had this ability to choose the right people at the right time. She could always find somebody who knew somebody who was involved in whatever was needed. She was a master of getting the right people engaged in the organization. And that's an art, and it's a talent, and it's having humility.*
>
> — Cathy Bernard, Imagination Stage VP board of trustees, entrepreneur, philanthropist

The Wrap

The entrepreneurial trait we identified and focused on in this chapter was:

- "People" people – they engage the right people to help them.

People are the heart of any organization, but particularly nonprofit organizations. They are the soul of the company and the engine that gets the work done. It seems obvious that having the right people doing the work is critical to an organization's success, and yet many nonprofit **managers** don't prioritize empowering and engaging their associates. **Entrepreneurial leaders**, on the other hand, recognize, empower, listen to and encourage employees. It is as important as keeping and growing your audiences for the long term. In fact, more important. You need the best employees to keep the most engaged audiences. The people are the points of connection for the work.

Entrepreneurial leaders need the right people to achieve their visions. They must attract, retain and grow the best. Maintaining a culture of transparency fosters loyalty and trust across the organization's DNA. Transparency is supported through a process of de-siloing and creating a flatter structure for greater efficiency.

Discussion Questions For Those Starting Or Growing Entrepreneurial Leadership

- Starters:
  - What do you think is the importance of getting the right people in your organization (*on the bus*) in order to accomplish your vision?
  - Have you ever been asked what *you* think at work?
  - What are meaningful ways to celebrate an associate's contributions to an organization?
  - How will you develop communication systems that are transparent and equitable?
- Adapters:
  - Have you asked associates what they think?
  - Is there a system for celebrating success to inspire associates throughout the year?
  - Is your organization's culture transparent?
  - Do you have communication pathways so that everyone knows where the organization is going and understands how their work contributes to its success?

- How do you create linkages between your staff's work to the strategic plan and annual goals of the organization?
- Is your organization working in tight departments with closed doors and blocked-off computer folders?
- How might you flatten your organization to gain more efficiency?

Trait 3

Igniting and Engaging: Entrepreneurial Leadership and the Board

Never doubt that a small group of thoughtful committed citizens can change the world; indeed, it's the only thing that ever has.

—Margaret Mead, anthropologist

An entrepreneurial leader knows that an efficient, effective engaged board is essential to ensuring a successful enterprise. While this is a core best practice, entrepreneurial leaders *must* engage in best practices to achieve their vision and the organization's mission.

Governance is the work of boards. Good governance ensures that the organization has the structures and practices in place that hold it accountable for good business practices based on responsible and ethical behavior that represents the community's interests. Some are fiduciary boards, some may be working boards and some may be a combination of both or hold other functions. Regardless, boards are not working alone – they are working in partnership with the nonprofit's leadership and staff.

Boards and governance are structures within corporations, and the vast majority of nonprofit organizations are corporations. In this chapter, we explain the traditional best practices of governance, and we spotlight the previously identified entrepreneurial traits:

- Market savvy – they can "read" the market to determine if this will sell;
- Promoters/advocates – they know how to successfully promote products/services;
- People – they engage the right people to help them.

As mission-based, nonprofit institutions, the boards of trustees or directors serve as representatives of their communities on a voluntary basis. But, as with their for-profit cousins, board members of nonprofit or for-profit organizations are responsible for the oversight of the business. As the board, they are legally responsible for ensuring that the organization remains true to its mission, safeguards its assets and operates in the public interest. The board is the first line of defense against fraud and abuse. Public trust and accountability are essential aspects of organizational viability, to ensure it achieves the social mission in a way that is respected by those whom the organization serves and the society in which it is located.[22]

Nonprofit governance has a dual focus: achieving the organization's social mission and ensuring the organization is viable. Both responsibilities relate to the fiduciary responsibility that a board provides financial oversight and advocacy for all external relationships, from fundraising to community business partnerships to elected and appointed officials.

Although the terms are often used interchangeably, there is a conceptual difference between a board of trustees (holding the trust of the community in their work often within the frameworks of serving as fiduciaries of a community trust) and a board of directors (responsible for directing the activities of a business). Interestingly, in the United States, each state's law dictates the minimal specifics of a board and its work. Each state may have differences in language. This is also true with respect to differences between countries, for example in some countries, there are different approaches to charities and NGOs (non-governmental organizations).

> *Here are examples from two states: New York and California are provided as they are two of the largest population states with long-standing nonprofit sectors, Maryland is included as it is the state in which Imagination Stage was founded.*
>
> *New York PC 1605 Consolidated Not – for – profit Law: "The members of the board of directors shall select annually from among themselves a chairman, a vice-chairman, a treasurer, and such other officers as the board may determine, and shall establish their duties as may be regulated by rules adopted by the board."*
>
> *California Law for Nonprofit Public Benefit Corporations, Directors and Management, General Provisions: Universal Citation: CA Corp Code § 5210 (2013) Each corporation shall have a board of directors. Subject to the provisions of this part and any limitations in the articles or bylaws relating to action required to be approved by the members (Section 5034), or by a majority of all members (Section 5033), the activities and affairs of a corporation shall be conducted and all corporate powers shall be exercised by or under the direction of the board. The board may delegate the management of the activities of the corporation to any person or persons, management company, or committee however composed, provided that the activities and affairs of the corporation shall be managed and all corporate powers shall be exercised under the ultimate direction of the board.*
>
> — Amended by Stats. 1996, Ch. 589, Sec. 4. Effective January 1, 1997

When creating a nonprofit corporation, the articles of incorporation and bylaws are filed with the secretary of state in the state of operation. This allows the government to evaluate both the purpose of the business as articulated in the Articles and the legal compliance of the structures of governance identified in the Bylaws. Bylaws set the framework of operations for a board. This includes how often the board meets, what constitutes a quorum, how the committee or other smaller group structures are organized and how long someone can serve on the board. It also defines who the officers are, what their roles and responsibilities will be and for how long. For all board members, term limits are a best practice. It prevents a culture of "it's always been this way" and allows new voices to enter the room. This is what keeps a board alive and meets the needs of the community.

As organizations move from their initial founding board and governance structures, structures forged at the organization's creation and filing of the articles of incorporation and bylaws, organizations will grow and evaluate their bylaws to meet the needs of their current business. To wit, there are best practices and systems that create strong board ecologies.

It is often asked, "**How many people should be on your board?**" There is no magic number, but there are legal minimums required depending on the state in which the organization is incorporated. These minimums do not reflect best practice or excellence; they are simply the legal minimum for nonprofit oversight.

Some believe that boards are **just a "waste of time."** Citing that they can be inefficient and ineffective and that they are not essential to a nonprofit's success. **We totally disagree** with this perspective. Our experience is exactly the reverse: boards are essential. **If board members are unproductive, it is often because staff leadership is inefficient, ineffective and wastes board members' time.** We suspect that some nonprofit leaders are overwhelmed by the work of governance or by sharing leadership of the organization with a strong board because it feels that their authority is potentially diminished.

We believe that **board members are the lifeblood of the organization**, second only to staff associates. A well-functioning board helps determine the well-being of the organization and helps ensure the furtherance of its mission. Board and staff, working in harmony, are the nonprofit's most powerful tool. They represent the difference between a functioning nonprofit and a supremely successful nonprofit. What's more: it's the law!

Nonprofits are granted 501c3 status on the understanding that they are meeting a genuine public interest and that they are overseen by a board of volunteers who are legally responsible for ensuring that the organization stays true to its mission and safeguards its assets. A board's fiduciary oversight responsibility includes approval of strategic **policy, planning and budget** decisions including setting direction and strategy, monitoring financial performance and **executive leadership evaluation.** Finally, board members are **advocates**, the **ultimate champions and ambassadors** of the nonprofit. They advocate on its behalf, they market and they bring the resources necessary to sustain the organization.

The entrepreneurial leader, one who knows that people are their strongest asset, prioritizes governance and cultivates an entrepreneurial board.

Too many nonprofit leaders and staff members decry board members (internally and externally) as being unproductive and unsupportive of the organizations they serve. **This needs to stop.** While it is imperative that board members "act like adults" by being proactive: looking for ways to help the organization, staff needs to remember that board members have full-time responsibilities outside the 501c3 and need staff support in the form of oral and written reminders of ways board members can help. Board members also need tools to help them maximize their effectiveness. This chapter examines ways to ensure **engagement.**

At Imagination Stage, in times of turmoil, and most recently during the COVID-19 pandemic when difficult decisions had to be made regarding furloughs and lay-offs, the staff knew that the board was "with them all the way" and helping as best they could. The **board president attended staff meetings** and co-presented with staff leadership about difficult decisions. Thus, staff associates understood that decisions had been deeply considered with the guidance of board leadership. It was also clear that the board was deeply committed and involved in their welfare and was working with staff leadership to help steer the ship through troubled waters. It was reassuring.

To ensure that a board is a productive partner, **We suggest that 10 percent of a leader's time be devoted to strategic and tactical** prospecting, engagement and management. Similarly, staff associates must adopt board management practices and tools that ensure board members practice appropriate fiduciary oversight. Simple strategies, which we detail below, will ensure that the organization is well served by its board. This chapter lays out a tool box of strategies for entrepreneurial staff leaders as it pertains to cultivating and building a board, as well as maintaining that board.

Cultivating and Building a Board

While you might only be required to have a small, three-person board of directors, it isn't the most strategic way to run a nonprofit corporation. Yes, staying with only a few individuals might allow for a simple system of power and control over the organization, but it loses the point of having a board of directors: creating connections and engaging stakeholders in your community.

Maintaining a breadth of perspectives across a diversity of community stakeholders is essential. There are phrases that underscore myths used in board management, one of which is "give or get." This concept is an articulation of engagement expectations that often predicate a mindset of cash (give your cash or get cash from someone else). However, that is not the wise practice in the twenty-first century if the board is to truly represent the community. Not everyone has to "pay" in cash, but engagement and advocacy on behalf of the organization are always expected. Cultivating individuals with some tangible offering, be it wealth or wisdom, is important. However, **critical** to a successful board, is pulling together a group of individuals all of whom have a passion for the mission of the institution, its work and its impact.

Maintaining a Board

While the day-to-day, week-to-week best practices are outlined in the case study of Imagination Stage, the most important thing is maintaining the engagement of the board. Excited board members easily attract new, curious board member "wanna-bes."

Engaging a board is a passion for the entrepreneurial leader who lives to involve the organization's stakeholders. In this instance, engagement means providing clear communication of work, impact and expectations. Weekly communications of activities and work are essential for keeping the organization front-of-mind, but so are meaningful opportunities for mission-focused interactions. (See Appendix I for a sample weekly board brief.) For a theatre, that might be attending a performance. For a museum, it might be attending an educational event around an exhibition. Engaging in the mission results in meaningful engagement on committees, for example, facilities, fundraising or finance.

> *Why join a board? To make a difference!*
>
> *I remember one discussion with a prospective board member who served on at least one national board that required him to fly to board meetings. It was a very prestigious board and one he thought would be a lot of fun. And yet, he concluded that he was not happy with the experience; he felt the organization was only "after my money." He was happy to be a financial contributor – but he was a very successful businessman and thought he could do much more to help the organization. He subsequently joined our board, and I worked hard to ensure that we involved him as an advisor in our business ventures, which really helped us tremendously, and let him feel that we "saw" him in his entirety – not just as a wallet.*
>
> *Stephen T. Hayes was another board member, who also sat on highly prestigious national boards, surprised me by remaining engaged on ours. I asked him why he bothered with Imagination Stage when he was involved in boards at a much higher level. He responded: "I feel I can make a difference here." And he could, and he did. He became a President of the organization, and one of the greatest.*
>
> — Bonnie Fogel, founder and executive director

CASE STUDY: IMAGINATION STAGE: ENTREPRENEURIAL GOVERNANCE IS IN THE RELATIONSHIPS

In many ways, success in **board governance is about relationships.** (See Appendix E for a board management and cultivation tool kit.) Cultivating the relationships among the board and between the board and the staff is a crucial aspect of building a harmonious "marriage" or partnership for years to come. Oftentimes, it's a feeling, a knowing, a sense that there is trust and respect among leadership staff and board associates. Not one dissimilar to the feeling you might get in more personal relationships – both romantic and platonic. At Imagination Stage, there is a long history of trust and respect developing into sustaining friendships. One hopes that strong relationships that benefit the smooth running of the nonprofit develop between and among staff and board leadership. But hope is not a strategy. Beyond "hope," **strategies *can* be adopted to support successful relationships.**

In the beginning, many nonprofits simply focus on staying alive. This was certainly true for BAPA/Imagination Stage. In the early days, **our nonprofit had a dream, but we didn't have a plan.** We especially didn't have a plan for our board. We all muddled along together, discussing our opportunities and challenges together.

As the organization matured, so did an understanding that to offer effective (and legally mandated) oversight Imagination Stage's governance model needed to evolve to create processes and systems for deep engagement and organizational understanding. A clear delineation of responsibilities was essential to prevent board member burnout and micro-management of staff. We recognized that to maintain our nonprofit status legally and to retain the community's trust, we had to ensure the comprehensive and fiduciary oversight of a highly credible board, which became a high priority.

Subsequently, our staff/board culture developed to where it is today: a group of community representatives who bring huge resources to the organization. We believe that our staff/board interactions represent a valuable give and take of ideas and strategies leading to the benefit of the organization.

> *What I love most about Imagination Stage is their intentionality on IDEA. They have always led the way in ensuring that their facility and classes were accessible for students with physical disabilities. With the expansion of the social justice and emotional support work that we conduct with Theatre for Change, and the expansion of programming in DC public and charter schools, we are ensuring inclusion and equity across various socioeconomic levels. And the casting alone for all of the shows produced at Imagination Stage displays the diverse spectrum of race, national origin, age, religion, gender/transgender/non-binary, etc. on stage for children to embrace as the norm.*
>
> — Kim Woodson Barnette, PhD, Imagination Stage board president (2022–25), project manager for LMI's team at NASA supporting inclusion, diversity equity and accessibility initiatives within their science mission directorate

The culture of shared leadership predominates. That said, there are clear lines of authority.

Imagination Stage focuses board member responsibilities on **policy, planning, budgeting and advocacy. Artistic and educational vision and its management** being the provenance of staff. This split recognizes the legal, fiduciary oversight authority of the board to operate the nonprofit in the community interest.

In terms of personal leadership responsibilities, the nonprofit **staff leader** is hired by the board and authorized by the board to carry out day-to-day management duties and to ensure that the mission and the vision of the organization are top-of-mind in decision-making. However, intentional supervision is necessary for creating an effective board management model. Chief executives work directly with board officers regularly. During my tenure at Imagination Stage, the board president was a consistent collaborator.

The board is legally in charge. In joint appearances, such as board meetings, special events and advocacy opportunities, staff should always defer to the board. For instance, at a board meeting, the **board president** opens, runs and closes the meeting. As executive director, I would provide context for areas for discussion if appropriate, as would the artistic director for areas under her purview.

Working with any board requires unwavering belief in the concept that the board's work as a community representation model is vital to the well-being of the nonprofit. As is an ongoing commitment to the board as an entity and to its individual members. The authenticity of the original engagement of the board member and the continuing need for that board member, not because they check a box, but because they represent a needed voice and resource, is the Golden Rule for board engagement.

The board as an entity should be managed by the governance committee (GC), should your organization have one, sometimes named the nominating committee. This committee should consider annually if the board has helped the organization meet its policy, planning, budgetary and advocacy goals for the year. The committee should also evaluate if the board make-up reflects the diversity of the community, and should evaluate the bylaws on a frequent, three- or five-year basis, to ensure they meet the legal and operational needs of the organization.

Leadership staff, along with board leadership, should check in with each board member on an annual basis to ensure that they feel they are contributing to meeting the mission and vision of the nonprofit. This should be tied to their annual engagement agreement, which Imagination Stage crafted with each board member by the end of the first quarter. One of the significant ways members engage is through committees. Board members should be asked annually on which committee or task force they wish to serve. One shouldn't assume, for instance, that a banker wants to serve on the finance committee – the banker may have joined your board hoping for a distraction from money matters. And one shouldn't assume that a member who represents a particular community wishes to focus only on work that serves that community.

SHARED LEADERSHIP CREATES INSTITUTIONAL SUCCESS

The board and staff leadership of the organization must define what success is. This is different for every organization, and it changes as the organization grows. Hence, success could be any of the following, or some combination, depending upon the maturity of your nonprofit:

- **Survival:** sufficient funding to keep the organization afloat,
- **A culture** that listens to its community and offers programs and services commensurate with needs and desires,
- A growing and **satisfied client** base as demonstrated by increased revenues,
- Community **understanding of the value** of the organization's work,
- Staff/board **satisfaction that the vision, mission, programs** of the organization are being met and that its patrons are very well-served,
- A **stable financial base** that assures staff, board and community that the organization will continue to provide its programs into the future,
- The **human capacity** needed to meet its mission,
- Work that is **fully reflective of its community** (as well as a board and staff that are also reflective of the community),
- The organization is seen to conduct itself with **integrity** and is considered to be **honest** and **authentic** by its patrons and its associates, and
- The organization **values and respects its staff associates** and prioritizes their needs.

After 40-plus years in business, those are the markers of a successful, entrepreneurial nonprofit. In many ways, Imagination Stage is an institutional success. Imagination Stage is:

- a nationally recognized multi-disciplinary, **Professional Theatre for Young Audiences** that offers high-caliber theatre arts training and opportunities for children aged 18 months to 18 years;
- reaching nearly **100,000 children and families** each year in the metropolitan region;
- developing a deep appreciation of theatre arts, while **building a sense of self** and community;
- expanding its seminal **Theatre for Change** program, which works with local jurisdictions and nonprofit partners to help mitigate burgeoning social justice issues affecting young people;
- **reflective of the community** in terms of the work it does and the composition of its board; and
- never stops looking for new ways to meet its mission in a changing world. The journey never ends.

The success of Imagination Stage rests on the work of brilliant, committed staff associates with a clear vision and mission and the programming skills to ensure the mission was met. And none of the major evolutions of Imagination Stage would have been possible absent the **significant** involvement (and engaged encouragement) of board leadership, for example, since 1979:

- Adding to its baseline theatre education platform by including children with **access and inclusion** needs,
- **Opening a professional theatre** at a local shopping center,
- Building a **permanent home** in a public parking garage in an urban center,
- **Incorporating Imagination Stage DC** (a second establishment) in **Washington, DC**, and
- Creating **Theatre for Change** – social justice programming.

CREATING A BOARD AND ONGOING PROSPECTING

We knew that it was a best practice to begin with a representation of those who benefited from the programs our nonprofit provided. First and last, Imagination Stage board members always understood and experienced the importance of the arts, in general, and theatre, specifically, for children.

Beyond simply finding individuals who understood the importance of the arts for children, creating a diverse board – for us – was also (and should be!) a no-brainer. Nonprofits bring specific programs to the community that the community lacks. Often, they ensure that essential human needs are met. Board members should reflect the breadth of the community served in all perspectives (not just race or gender). If, like Imagination Stage, you are creating education programs with K-12 schools, representatives from that part of the workforce community should have a voice at the table.

Sadly, this is not always the case. Often, boards are created with the specific and narrow goal of installing wealthy people who can support the financial needs of the organization. This funding-driven practice of board engagement is a very narrow view of what a board should be. Entrepreneurial leaders recognize that people represent all manner of resources for a board and they strategically seek out those who can help. A board should be populated with people who bring *resources,* not necessarily monetary, to the organization. The following demonstrates how we at BAPA/Imagination Stage cultivated our board.

- **Community served:** our first board members were **parents of the children** for whom we were offering programs. We continue to prioritize this group.

- **Access and inclusion:** when we added programs for **children with access and inclusion** needs (then referred to as disabilities), we made sure we had people on the board who represented that community.
- **Professional diversity:** our organization was always built on the premise that earned income was more reliable than contributed, so we looked to add **business people** to the board who would bring a business, profit-driven sensibility. To find businesspeople, we joined the local Chamber of Commerce and in a short time added several people from that source.
- **Gender diversity:** because we were a female-run, and majority female staff, we **intentionally cultivated men and male-identified individuals** to our board to add their perspectives to the work.
- **Spectrum of ages:** we found that by doing so, it helped with programming. Parents and caregivers of children from early – childhood to teenage years to grandparents were included.
- **Income diversity:** as noted earlier, we have always looked to get the "right people on the bus" – so eloquently coined by Jim Collins in *Good to Great.* First, people who represented a resource we needed. Often the people we needed did not have personal wealth. Although at Imagination Stage, there was a "give/get" board dues structure, there's flexibility to recognize key non-financial contributions as equitable to cash. We do always ask that everyone give something from their own/not their business pockets. Invariably, through our nominations pipeline, Imagination Stage found that those contributing resources other than financial, do as much, if not more to move the organization toward meeting its mission.
- **Racial and ethnic diversity:** our goal has always been that our board reflect the diversity of our community – and Imagination Stage has been successful in attracting and engaging a racially diverse board. Because we live in a metropolitan area, we have a very diverse population from which to discover new board member talent.
- **Political diversity:** this may not often be considered but is vitally important for the well-being of an organization. The culture of nonprofits may easily attract people who are more likely to vote left of center, but we know there are people of all political persuasions who want the arts for their children. It is essential that all be represented. Imagination Stage has been particularly effective in cultivating a board with significant resources on both sides of the political spectrum. (See Trait 5: "The Power of Your Voice and Advocacy" for a full discussion of this.)

The following are three examples of non-monetary contributions of Imagination Stage board members:

1. ***Mary.*** *Mary's presence on our board was critical to the success of our growing Deaf Access Program. A deaf educator, Mary's presence gave us credibility in the deaf population AND gave staff associates insight into the community they were serving.*
2. ***Antonio.*** *A leader in the Hispanic community, Antonio's presence on the board added to our credibility as we grew our programs for Latino children and families. And Antonio helped us launch our Theatre for Change programming and expand it to achieve a national presence.*
3. ***Kim.*** *A leader with deep roots in the Washington DC Community, Kim brought credibility to our board as we established a presence in that City. Her high profile, friends, political connections and knowledge of the political realities of the City assured us of a successful launch.*

Over the history of Imagination Stage, the organization has often advanced due to the non-financial resources of board members or others in the community. If you build a strong nonprofit that does exemplary and authentic work, money will follow. First and last you are asking them because they share your passion for your mission and vision for the community.

MARRIAGE AND THE "HAPPILY-EVER-AFTER": BOARD SUCCESS AT IMAGINATION STAGE

In its 40-year history, BAPA/Imagination Stage, there have been many times when board members either led the way or followed in a close advisory/support role as staff leadership plotted a new course which led to a stronger, more inclusive, organization that better served its ever-widening community. Because of the nature of our board and the culture that we cultivated, we were able to enjoy many successes. Such as:

- **Access and inclusion:** board leadership (President **Bobbie Gottschalk** specifically) was essential to adapting the policies of Bethesda Academy of Performing Arts (BAPA) to welcome children with Access and Inclusion needs. Programs for children with physical and/or cognitive support needs and children who were deaf or hard of hearing followed and became national models for integration.
- **Saving our first home from demolition:** we discovered that our leased home in an elementary school was about to be razed to make room for a new high school. Board President **Nancy Greenspan** led the way to get this threat overturned.
- **Our first theatre home:** we followed the example of Kansas City's **The Coterie** and asked the owners of the White Flint shopping center to allow us to use one of their closed spaces to start a professional theatre for young audiences. The

idea came from staff leadership, but Board President **Jerry Morenoff** led the negotiations with the owners. This successful venue led to the organization's decision to find a new home that would accommodate the growing success of the professional theatre.

- **Our permanent home:** the board led the way, specifically Vice President **Gene Smith**, found the space, negotiated with the county to achieve it, worked with the architect to design it and the construction company to build it. Board President **Robby Brewer** worked on the financing and the real estate requirements. This "set the stage" for the stabilization of the organization and its institutional status today. **Cathy Bernard** used her political entre and building management savvy to help us achieve significant cost savings.
- A **second incorporation:** Board President **Jane Fairweather** and President-Elect **Kim Alfonso** worked to achieve the incorporation of the organization in DC, ensuring delivery of increased programming to the children of DC, a separate funding path and creating a pathway for a second permanent home in that city.

There were also many significant programs, projects and advances which did not rise to the level of evolutions but made a big difference to the work and success of the organization and owed their advancement to board engagement. There were also "near-death threats" that were overcome with the help of board leadership. For example, when the county was going to tear down the school in which BAPA and other organizations operated. The chair of the board, Nancy Greenspan, led the charge to get the county council to come to see the building and created a press event with a "community hug" around the building. The council decided to let the building and its occupants stay. All that being said, the message is that a deeply committed board – one that understands your mission and vision – is essential for your nonprofit to succeed.

GROWING A BOARD: FROM PROSPECTING TO DATING TO MARRIAGE

Engagement is an entrepreneurial strategic practice for us. **In examining how to grow a board and keep them active and engaged,** we liken the journey to one of **dating to marriage (and potentially, divorce).** For instance, we can break down the process similarly:

- Finding a potential match,
- Effective dating and courtship,
- Marry and stay "happily-ever-after,"
- Or … divorce.

Getting a prospect to consider joining a board is oftentimes not difficult – people are usually flattered to be asked. If your mission is strong, your service is essential and if the right person asks the prospect will probably say "yes." People like to be asked; they like that their value is recognized. That said, be careful who you ask! Remember that your nonprofit has something of value to offer too. So don't roll over like a dog that wants its stomach rubbed if someone shows an interest. **It's a two-way street.** Think carefully about whether the prospect will be a good fit (just like you would a potential romantic partner!), and ensure that they fully understand and agree to the commitment before you propose. **Put a lot of thought into finding a good match before you start dating. Measure twice; cut once.**

> *Bonnie's secret sauce was that she groomed and relied upon her board members to be true partners in the success of the organization. These efforts took a lot of time and patience, but she always believed the payoff would be worth it.*
>
> — Patrick O'Neil, Esq., Imagination Stage board president, 2019–22; attorney, Lerch, Early and Brewer

PROSPECTING IS ON-GOING

Finding prospects shouldn't be a once-a-year thing. Too many nonprofits fling a nominating committee together a month before the annual meeting and hope they will come up with some good names. **That doesn't work.**

Instead, **prospecting must be an ongoing, year-round activity** and one that is always top-of-mind for board and staff associates. Effective prospecting demands a structured and disciplined process. This is a "full board" responsibility. As such, at Imagination State, the GC was tasked with guiding and fulfilling that responsibility.

At Imagination Stage, we used the following approach to prospecting where GCs were advised to adopt the following practices such that board prospecting gets the attention it deserves:

- **The governance committee** meets at least six times a year with board prospecting always on the agenda. GC members are expected to bring prospects to the table at each meeting and staff assigned to the GC should maintain a prospect list that is regularly updated. Continual prospecting is critical because, once identified, ideally there is a six-month "dating" period where the prospect is invited to activities, identified below.

- Every **board committee** meeting should make a practice of asking their members: "Did you meet anyone who could be a good board member whose name we can recommend to the Governance Committee?"
- **Every board meeting** should include a request for prospects. Board members should be reminded at each meeting that identifying new prospects is one of their responsibilities. Board members are also advised in their orientation and board responsibilities handbook that "replacing themselves" is part of this responsibility!

When it comes to prospecting, especially as an ongoing process, it can feel daunting. And it is, in a lot of ways. However, there are some avenues that you can explore to make the task seem less cumbersome.

LOOK TO WHO YOU ALREADY KNOW

- At Imagination Stage, **board committees and task forces** were board members and "lay people." We regularly invited non-board members to join these entities. Be sure to check here first!
- **Former board members.** If your organization has existed for many years, and if you have rigorous term limits on board membership, be sure to see if some board members who have cycled off might be good candidates.
- **Staff leadership should ask staff associates** regularly: "which of your clients, parents, users are particularly passionate about the mission and have resources that can help support our work."
- **Development staff** must regularly scrutinize their lists, from individuals to corporate or business partners or sponsors, for prospects who have self-identified by making generous donations to the cause, communicating regularly and/or showing up for events.
- **Elected officials.** Many boards include elected officials. Some boards even have "spots" on their boards held for elected officials because the government wants monitoring representation on this board. Think carefully about this. From a fundraising point of view, it is not a good idea because elected officials may not make contributions. But it may be that having a county councilor on your board would be a helpful resource for legal or advocacy reasons. If votes are involved, elected officials who are board members or similarly closely tied to your organization would have to recuse themselves from a vote.
- **Appointed officials.** These would be the heads of agencies, appointed by city, county or state elected leadership. They can be helpful to your board. Mostly, these officials prefer not to join a board, they are too busy and they don't want to commit to one of many good causes. Again, while Imagination Stage has

not had appointed officials on our board, we have retained close relationships with both elected and appointed officials.

- **Spouses, partners, family members!** Often the person you identify for your board is simply too busy. However, their spouse or partner, or another family member, may not be and has many of the same relationships and resources that brought the original prospect to your attention. And the new prospect may have one additional resource: much more time to devote to your cause.

If the organization has a **Strategic Plan**, and/or a comprehensive annual plan **that identifies programming priorities** (and it should!), it is a good practice to prospect for **new members who can help support those strategic priorities.**

However, we have never agreed with the recommendation that a grid be maintained as a sole determinant of which areas of the operation particularly need help: legal, fundraising, marketing, legislative advocacy, human resources, etc. Instead, as with hiring staff associates, we follow **Jim Collins's** mantra: **"First, get the right people on the bus ..."** If you have the right people on the board, those with passion and the time to dedicate to moving your organization forward, the rest will fall into place. **The most essential board prospect's skill and talent is that they have a passion for your organization.** These board members will find the resources you need if they don't personally have the skills. Also, board member prospects may be insulted if they think they have only been invited to a board to save the organization money by using their professional skills without paying for them.

As noted earlier, **never invite a board member to join the board simply because they have financial resources.** Of course, we must have board members who can support us, but limiting the form of support can be insulting. Unless you represent that very small number of boards that exist with the sole goal of providing funds for the organization, and board members agree to this when they sign on, this is not the way to go. Find out what your **prospect's passion** is, and if it aligns with that of your organization, likely you have a match.

As noted earlier, **finding a match is not difficult.** Most people want to be involved in something that is bigger than themselves. **People are always looking to add meaning to their lives, they also are looking for fun!** If you can provide both, you have a very good chance of getting excellent board members. Just be very careful before you start to date that your prospect is, in fact, a prospect!

EFFECTIVE DATING AND COURTSHIP: YOU'VE FOUND A MATCH, NOW WHAT?

Don't be in a rush! Like any marriage, you want this to last and you have to be sure you have made a good choice. You don't want to waste time and effort on a board member who isn't going to work out. Of course, this still happens no matter how diligent you are, but do your best to preclude that situation. Take your time. **Ideally, the dating-to-marriage pipeline takes six to nine months in the governance or nominating committee process.**

You have found a prospect who has the attributes you are looking for, and has indicated an interest in being "more involved." Using the "**being involved**" language is a good way to position yourself for a variety of scenarios should the board prospect not work out on closer examination. Your conversation might go like this:

- **Nonprofit leader:** "You seem to really enjoy your engagement with our organization, might you be interested in becoming more involved?"
- **Prospect:** "I think so, what might that entail ...?"
- **NPL:** "I'd like to set up a meeting (a first date!) to talk that through with you ... to discuss what involvement might look like."

Dating Steps

1. **Inviting a prospect on a date:** the board member or the staff associate with the relationship invites the prospect to coffee or lunch for an informal discussion "to explore your interest in getting more involved ..." Depending upon the circumstances, the board member or staff associate might also invite another person from the board or staff to that date.
2. **Prior to the first date:** if circumstances allow, invite the prospect to attend an opening night or another special event. At this event, the prospect is welcomed by staff associates and hand-picked board members and made to feel valued.
3. **The first date:** you have a checklist of things you want to talk about, but **the single most important thing to achieve is a connection.** It's a date, if it goes well, all else will follow.

Your Dating Checklist

- **Re-establish why you are meeting.** Note that they came to your attention because they are such a good advocate, user and donor.
- **Listen first/share second:** ask the prospect to talk about **themselves** and **their experience** at your nonprofit. It is very important to give the prospect the opportunity to talk (it's amazing how often this doesn't happen – that the staff associate JUST talks to the person about how amazing the organization is) and share their perspective. **Show them, by listening**, that who they are and what they believe in is valued.

- Ask how their experience with your nonprofit has had meaning for them and their family. **Notice** how this meshes with the mission of the organization. Respond to what they say. "I'm so glad that _____ resonated with you, it will make our team happy to hear this."
- **Only after the prospect has fully shared** their interest should you ask whether they have an interest in getting more closely involved with the organization. [**If the answer is "Yes I would!"** Now is your chance to give a short presentation (five minutes max) on the organization's mission, vision, current status, challenges and opportunities for future growth.]
- **Ask if they have any questions** about the organization.
- **Clarify:** clearly state the benefits of closer involvement with your organization. To the person themselves, to their friends, to their family. Reiterate that this will be a meaningful experience and "fun!" **Fun is not to be overlooked.** After all, fun is the essence of our practice and our **product. Board** members are looking for meaning, and they are looking for fun. Some also want to improve their social life, make new friends, business connections, engage in different ways than their current lives allow. Be sure to try to get a sense of what your prospect needs.
- **Ask:** "given this understanding of our organization, how do you feel you might best be engaged?" Don't assume anything, you may be surprised!
- **Ask:** "would you consider exploring the opportunity to join the board?"

If the answer is "yes!", it's a good idea to ask "why?" Ask the candidate to put into words why they want to work with you for the benefit of the community. Then explain that the on-boarding process gives the candidate the opportunity for a closer association with the board before committing. Explain that the process takes a few months but that there is plenty of time before the next slate of board prospects is nominated. In the meantime, recommend that the prospect:

1. Join a board committee,
2. Attend special events as our guest,
3. Meet with one of our GC members who will serve as a mentor and answer questions that will arise. Wrap the conversation by reiterating that this process assures that both parties get to know each other comprehensively before a formal commitment is made, and
4. Take home and study a portfolio of reading materials on the organization, especially the latest financial report.

From here, it will be important to foster a relationship of transparency as it pertains to finances, expectations and overall commitment. This is done to ensure that key questions and concerns are answered prior to a firm commitment being made.

Your Post-Dating Checklist

- **Provide an orientation to the organization's financials.** It is critical that board prospects understand the financial situation of the organization they are considering. Most board prospects do not come from the nonprofit world and they may be shocked at how close to the edge we often live. You don't want your board prospects to be surprised at your financials after they have committed to join you.
- **Prevent confusion on the fundraising expectation.** If your nonprofit has a minimum "**Give or Get**" financial goal for each board member, be sure to underscore it at this meeting. **Make it very clear what the expectations are** and ask: "is this realistic for you?" It is important to note that a "Give or Get" model is tied to a finance-only oriented board. As noted earlier, wisdom is needed as are community connections and passion for the work. However, in the event that your prospect is being invited onto the board to serve as a non-financial resource, you need to make it clear that they must make some contribution annually, even if it is $20. **Every board member must make a personal, financial contribution.** And, those board members whose companies make their contribution for them should **also give personally** to validate their commitment. If the "Give or Get" is not comfortable for the board prospect, ask: "can you tell me the amount you would be comfortable pledging, and/or get from other sources." **It's hard to talk about money; it's even harder asking for it. But talking about it upfront is essential and will prevent confusion later.**
- **Follow up.** Put a date on the calendar to follow up in a few months, a time that is one month ahead of the board nomination process.

This whole process may seem overly comprehensive and time intensive, but, ultimately, it will save a lot of aggravation if both parties fully understand the board member's commitment from the get-go.

Remember, you are not a supplicant. This is a two-way street. Don't just propose board membership quickly because the prospect seems willing. **Date first.** The prospect may not end up being right for your organization, they may be too busy; they may not be able to commit financial or other support. Best for both parties to have a full understanding of the ability of the prospect to commit before you propose.

Sometimes, the conversation will lead to a mutually agreed decision that the time to join the board is not right. And, the prospect may become an even bigger advocate and supporter as a result of the conversation, because they have learned more about you and the organization. This has happened to Imagination Stage several times. **Your biggest funders, advisors, supporters ... are not always your board members!**

PROPOSE, MARRY AND REVEL IN THE "HAPPILY-EVER-AFTER"

The dating went well. It's time to propose! Think about this step as a job interview with ample opportunity for both sides to ask questions. Invite your prospect to coffee, lunch or a meeting at the nonprofit. The board president, chair of the GC and staff leadership should attend this meeting.

At the meeting, share again the **roles and responsibilities of board members.** Orally and in writing.

Explain that board members are considered **champions and advocates** for the organization and that you hope that they will continue as such long after their board terms have ended. **Indeed, one way to evaluate the success of your governance operation is to determine how many board members are still engaged with the organization!**

In this phase, questions are asked and answered by both "sides" and the prospect is informed of the board term and the nomination process. In regard to board terms, we advise a **three-year term or something near that number**, with a second three-year term possible – if mutually beneficial.

NOTE: The **nomination process starts in the GC** where a slate of candidates is drawn up, approved by the GC and then recommended by them to the executive committee. Assuming the executive committee has no issues with the candidates, the **slate is emailed to the full board ahead of the annual general meeting.** Board members are asked to be in touch with the GC chair ahead of the meeting if they have any questions regarding any candidate. The slate is offered and voted on at the **annual general meeting** and the new board members join the board at the beginning of the organization's new fiscal year, following an orientation.

Marriage ... and "Happily Ever After" is accomplished through an intentional and rigorous process for orienting and engaging board members throughout their tenure. (A Toolkit and more information about this process is detailed in Appendix E.)

KNOWING WHEN TO DIVORCE

Inevitably, some marriages do not enter or remain in that Happily-Ever-After stage; instead, they end in divorce. This is also true of some board relationships.

"Dead Wood"

Too many nonprofits have **"dead wood" on their boards** for a multitude of reasons: (1) he pays his dues; (2) everyone likes her; (3) we don't want anyone to be upset ...

all of which are specious arguments, and just an excuse for not doing the hard work. No one likes confrontation or dis-harmony. But it is the job of a leader to deal with it. It is especially important if the bylaws allow for a set number of board members and this non-performing person is taking up a space that could be held by someone who will perform better. Like non-performing staff, when they don't meet their responsibilities, board members need to be cut adrift. **Everyone will be happier** when they are.

Of course, **you will want to handle this in the *nicest* possible way.** You are not angry; you are **understanding.** This was a volunteer assignment, and you **understand** when things change. None of us knows what the future may hold when we commit. This board member may be going through a rough patch at work or at home. This board member may come back or send another prospect your way. Or this board member may continue to be supportive in other ways.

So, what constitutes "dead wood"? It can't be "just a feeling." You need proof; proof that our GC's engagement grid provided (Appendix F). This is also your own assurance that you are not imagining that your board member is slipping in their engagement. A board member's failure to meet the basic requirements set out on the GC's engagement grid or tracking sheet is the backup you need for a conversation with the board member.

The Divorce Proceedings: A Step-By-Step Process

- First, the **governance chair**, on behalf of the committee, brings the non-engagement of a board member to the attention of the president. Examples of perceived non-engagement would be: (1) They have not attended board or committee meetings, (2) they have not made a financial contribution and/or (3) they have not been responsive to staff for input.
- Afterward, the **board president** sets up a meeting with the board member. The conversation might start with the board president noting that:

  It seems [name of organization] is not a priority for you anymore, we have noticed you haven't been attending board or committee meetings, etc. etc. Has something changed in your family or professional life that makes it more difficult for you to include (name of organization) in your schedule?
- (You have the **government engagement grid** in your back pocket if there is a disagreement on this point.)

Sometimes, a quiet conversation will bring the board member back into the fold. **Usually,** the board member and board leadership agree that the organization is no longer a priority and the board member should step down in favor of someone who has time and ability to contribute at accepted levels.

The two can come to a decision as to when the board member should retire from the board. Ideally, this happens at the end of the financial year. **Very occasionally**, board members do not respond to requests for meetings, phone calls, etc. In this case, a **brief letter should be sent to the board member simply thanking them for their service on the board and wishing them well.**

THE TROUBLEMAKER: FAILURE TO ENGAGE

Unlike the board member who has to be let go because they do not fulfill their fiduciary responsibilities, there may be a board member who is a trouble maker who negatively impacts board discussions or who is upsetting staff associates. Sometimes, you have to ask a board member to leave – even if they don't want to. The conversation above can be adapted with the expression "no longer a good fit" substituting for the "no longer a priority" statement.

If the person responsible for a negative environment is the board president or another member of board leadership, this is especially difficult to deal with. It's unusual but it happens. And it must be dealt with before the board is poisoned.

Sometimes the troublemaker is a productive board member who has a committee leadership position. Trouble can start when they move into a starring role, as they might not have the time or skills to be a committee leader.

In my experience, this happened when the board member came from a corporate background and never understood the nonprofit culture, certainly never embraced it. This lack of understanding and, ultimately, support for your organization's mission often rears its head in meetings that discuss finances. A nonprofit's "people first" culture may clash with the mentality of a board member from the for-profit sector, where profit is the motive. When this happens, a lot of listening, communicating and tact on both sides is required to achieve a peaceful resolution, and sometimes the divorce procedure should be followed.

Beyond the consideration of selecting the right prospects for your board, and keeping them engaged, there is also the notion of shared leadership and the role of the board president to consider.

SHARED LEADERSHIP AND THE "POWER" OF THE PRESIDENCY

The role of the board president is circumscribed. There are many things that are rote and that you will have written into your board handbook. That said, each board president brings their own interests and strengths to the role.

At Imagination Stage, it seems that we have always been lucky enough to have the right board president for "the moment!" Whether it was our founding board president who gave us the confidence to "dream big," or the president who pushed us to include those with disabilities, or the president who helped us negotiate for a theatre in a shopping mall or the president who helped us navigate the political and financing landscape when we established a permanent home ... or the president who helped position us for success in our creation of a new business in Washington DC, the list goes on.

And, while I say that we were "lucky," this has not simply happened by luck or coincidence. Imagination Stage presidents-elect are selected one year out, with the understanding that they will be elected the following year. They spend the year shadowing the current president, attending meetings with leadership staff and getting to understand the challenges and opportunities so that they hit the ground running. In the absence of the president, the president-elect steps in and may exercise the power and authority of the president when the president is absent or unable to act.

This selection of the president-elect is strategic. Every two years, the president's emeriti are invited by the current board president to a meeting to reconnect with each other and to get an update from staff leadership. At this meeting, the current board president will recommend the next president. The nomination and election of the president-elect is then the responsibility of the presidents emeriti. We like this practice exceedingly; it keeps the former presidents engaged and gives them an important responsibility while bringing in people outside of the current board dynamics.

The president is the executive head of the nonprofit and is responsible for its overall direction and ensures that the board meets its fiduciary responsibilities especially in terms of policy, planning and budgeting. The president also designates the staff leader to undertake the artistic and educational vision and its management of day-to-day activities and staff. First and last, the board president is the board's cheerleader, responsible for the engagement of the board. And, notably, their role is in title and function. Being president doesn't make your vote count any more than anyone else's. The board president and the staff executive(s) are each other's #1 ally. Hence, entrepreneurial leaders cultivate entrepreneurial mindsets with their boards.

A conversation with a president prior to their assumption of office can help them understand their role in achieving the entrepreneurial vision of the organization. I particularly admired the diligence of one president who after our meeting wrote his own goals for the year on an index card, which he diligently referenced regularly to ensure he was on task.

They were not board presidents, but these board and community leaders played remarkable roles in the success of Imagination Stage:

Gene Smith: board senior vice president: alerted the organization to the opportunity to build the permanent home in a county garage, masterminded every aspect of the development of the new Imagination Stage building with the architect, county government partners, financiers and leadership staff. All at no cost to the organization.

Cathy Bernard: board vice president: decades of excellent advice regarding business decision-making, real estate and finances backed up by major gifts.

Carol and Jim Trawick: Angel donors who paid off the outstanding deficit on the building. Carol Trawick also guided staff leadership for decades in community and political strategy and leverage.

The Wrap

Entrepreneurial traits we identified and focused on in this chapter were:

- Market savvy – they can "read" the market to determine if this will sell,
- Promoters/advocates – they know how to successfully promote products/services,
- People – they engage the right people to help them.

The board of directors is in charge of the organization and through their hiring and continued work with the leadership, organizations can thrive, strive or fail. Continual cultivation and maintenance of a board of directors is part of the work of a nonprofit organization, but it is all done with one end in mind: **fulfilling the mission**.

Cultivating an engaged and productive board should take time, and leaders should spend 10 percent or so of their weekly work engaged with the board. Some say, though, that it takes much more time. We would say it only takes more time if you don't recruit and cultivate the right board for the right job. Ultimately, when it comes to the board, it's important to remember that it is all about developing engaged board members through relationships.

- Relationships with your board members are no different than relationships with significant others in your life – you start with a cup of coffee;
- Intention, rigor and discipline are necessary to engage your board to reach their full potential;
- The board of directors is responsible and legally in charge of the organization, The collaboration between them, the staff and the community is essential for success; and

- The board president must be carefully and strategically chosen as their work as a leader and cheerleader sets the tone.

Discussion Questions For Starting Or Growing Entrepreneurial Leaders

- Starters:
  - Imagine a board that truly offers voices from the community that you need at your table. Who (generally) would you want to be there?
  - What resources (intellectual, financial, social, etc.) would you want them to contribute to the organization?
  - How should you structure your week/month/year to actively work with your board to accomplish your mission and strategic goals?
- Adaptors:
  - Consider your community, demographically, politically, and its dominant industries. Is your board representative of your community?
  - Consider your programs, do you have voices at the board table that provide perspectives that help you consider and make decisions?
  - Review your bylaws. What you would like to change after reading this chapter? Term limits? Annual agreements?
  - On a scale of 1–10, where is board engagement as a priority?
    - If you asked a random board member if they knew (a) what your organization was doing right now and (b) if they had attended the last program would they say yes?
  - How do you communicate with your board?

Trait 4

Making the Difference: Partnership and Community

Great things in business are never done by one person; they're done by a team of people.

—Steve Jobs, Apple co-founder, chairman and CEO

Partnerships and collaborations are an essential tool in the entrepreneurial leader's toolbox. Yet, partnerships and collaborations are not unique to nonprofit work, but those with an entrepreneurial mindset do them frequently with a goal to create something new, not just to share resources. They, in fact, engage five of the six entrepreneurial traits.

- **Visionary** – they identify opportunities in the nonprofit's community;
- **Creative and innovative** – they imagine new ways to provide new opportunities through innovative programming and services;
- **"People" people** – they engage the right people to help them;
- **Market savvy** – they can "read" the market to determine if this will sell;
- **Promoters/advocates** – they know how to successfully promote products/services.

Understanding the key principles of partnerships is necessary before engaging in these opportunities as an entrepreneur. Creating partnerships and collaborating with other businesses is common among most enterprises. For nonprofit arts and cultural organizations, this work is often mission-critical, if not mission-centric, and can offer opportunities through deeply engaging with their local community. These relationships provide brand, financial or impact opportunities to each enterprise that a nonprofit could not accomplish alone.

Sometimes people confuse partnerships with collaborations. A partnership is a formal joint venture that is contractually binding, whereas collaboration has a more informal cooperative framework with flexible relationships and structures. The focus is achieving shared goals through teamwork.

Whether standard or entrepreneurial, partnerships and collaborations are formal agreements between two companies or individuals to accomplish a purpose. The agreement may be informal, with terms agreed to in an email. However, most should be articulated through more formal documents. Critical to forming a clear and functional agreement is understanding the purpose of the partnership, the roles each partner is responsible for including decision-making power, resources and day-to-day responsibilities, and the timeline of engagement. If intellectual property is being created, a clear understanding of future interests needs to be articulated.

There are three distinct types of partnerships in the arts and cultural space. The first focuses on mission-centric activities. A well-documented model is in creative or artistic production. Arts organizations might co-produce a production with each entity sharing the process and the product within tightly negotiated terms. The second is administrative. Organizations can collaborate with shared resources, they might share a space, have shared services or offerings like ticketing software or even a health insurance plan, or they might split an administrative role, with two organizations hiring one person to do a specific role for both, like bookkeeping. The third most common partnership is found in marketing. Marketing collaborations and partnerships are common and frequent with organizations agreeing to cross-market their work to expand their reach. Some collaborations are small with a list-share or a cross-promotion. Some have more whimsy, for example, Imagination Stage partnered with the National Geographic Museum in Washington, DC to do a cross-blog review. A staff member from each organization attended the others' work and wrote a review on their blog. A more formal marketing partnership comes in the form of a media sponsorship, often within corporate sponsorship work. The National Geographic partnership is a standard partnership with a fun twist. While important to always engage these traditional paths, the key to engaging the entrepreneurial mindset is moving this work from a single dimension to a multiple dimension.

The most impactful and **entrepreneurial partnerships** will incorporate all three types: the partnership will engage in mission-centric activities, share resources across multiple departments and offer synergy across audiences, donors or other markets. Sometimes they may, together, reach out to new communities or create new programs to reach a new market and a Blue Ocean that could not be done alone. The best partnership will be mutually beneficial.

Partnerships Make the Difference

As Steve Jobs says: great things in business are never done by one person, no matter how brilliant that one person is – and Jobs was a brilliant entrepreneur – he would know. As an entrepreneurial nonprofit arts leader, it is essential that you involve every single member of your staff and board teams in your vision, philosophy and practice. Then, expand that thinking to the stakeholders in your community and especially to anyone with whom you can do business. Good partners can make a big difference. In fact, successful nonprofits are deeply integrated into their communities and in solid partnerships with many different community entities.

The key to success is synergy. Partners and collaborators must share a point of overlap in their mission or audience regardless of whether the partner is another nonprofit or a for-profit. For instance, you may ask yourself: Are we all working toward the same goal? Is there an overlap with the people we serve geographically, demographically or psychographically?

Furthermore, each organization must focus on its mission. Arts organizations make art. But in partnership with, for example, a homeless shelter or a prison, that work can expand outside our buildings and reach more people. And, successful organizations must meet market needs with a strong army of marketing and communications. Entrepreneurial organizations go beyond that need by expanding the market through unusual and visionary partnerships.

> *At Imagination Stage, it's always been about partnerships and relationships, both in the business community and in the government.*
>
> — Carol Trawick, entrepreneur and philanthropist, Jim and Carol Trawick Foundation

CASE STUDY: IMAGINATION STAGE – COMMUNITY AND PARTNERSHIPS AMPLIFY OPPORTUNITY

Imagination Stage's decades-long success is the result of a great foundational vision and mission backed by an entrepreneurial stance. Leadership's belief that partnerships with government entities, corporations/businesses, foundations and/or other nonprofits would result in Imagination Stage's ability to have a greater impact on our community was confirmed repeatedly. Especially for new outreach projects, we could be stronger and provide more impact to the community by working with other like-minded and sometimes powerful players. In almost all the Imagination Stage partnerships, the entrepreneurial vision preceded outreach to a potential partner.

For years, Imagination Stage worked very hard to overcome the perception that theatre was an elitist occupation and not a necessary part of every child's life. This perception was furthered by the fact that our location was in an upmarket part of the county. We spent decades building partnerships with police, libraries, recreation and parks, and the school system. Over time, we reached a place where these departments had heard of us and welcomed our programs as additions to their own work. For instance:

- One workshop series developed in partnership with the county's department of health and human services, empowers recently arrived migrant youth through the sharing of their stories.
- a series of workshops in partnership with DC Police Foundation and DC Metropolitan Police, uses improv and acting to bring together young people and DC law enforcement officers in conversations that foster trust and understanding.

This not only allowed us to expand our services to all areas of the community but also it pleased our elected and appointed officials and donors. So, add creating partnerships to your tool box!

The following partnerships resulted in expanded opportunities for children to have access to Imagination Stage, its theatre and its arts education programs and services. These relationships allowed us to serve new communities with new programs – which we could not undertake alone. And many of the programming expansions also resulted in new funding support – a win-win!

In every partnership, it was important that everyone felt they were benefiting from the collaboration.

GOVERNMENT PARTNERSHIPS

Through the decades, Imagination Stage has benefited significantly from government support for specific capital projects and for on-going operating funding. Built over time, this trusted relationship led to many partnerships that were mutually beneficial to Imagination Stage and to the government and of great value to the communities we both served. Significant ongoing partnerships include:

- A partnership with the **county government** established Imagination Stage's "Forever Home" in the lower levels of a county parking garage in downtown Bethesda. This assured Imagination Stage a sustainable home from which to offer and expand its programs. While Imagination Stage was responsible for $13M to cover the build-out of the space, the county supported the project with:
  - 42,000 sq. ft. facility located in a parking garage in a downtown area but with easy access for families, school trips and summer camp visits,
  - $1 per sq. ft. rent,
  - Utility fees paid by the county.
  - Some infrastructure upkeep by the county.

- Partnership with the **school system** and the **state department of education,** whereby third-grade Title 1 students from across the state (those who qualify for free and reduced meals) are provided free tickets to one show a season. The schools pay for the buses. The tickets are subsidized by a grant from the state which supports out-of-school-time experiences. Imagination Stage's education department works with the local school system to select a play that will support the school system's curriculum goals and supply teacher support materials that reflect local, state and federal requirements for academic learning.
- The long-standing relationship with the county **department of recreation** expanded into relationships with the department of **health and human services** and with **police departments** in Maryland and the District of Columbia leading to a partnership that established Imagination Stage's **Theatre for Change.**

Imagination Stage's **Theatre for Change** program brought social justice theatre productions and student learning experiences to junior and high school students and to incarcerated youth thanks to a partnership with school systems. For example,

- ***Oyéme! is*** a one-act touring play and post-play student activities depicting the trauma experienced by unaccompanied minors from Central America coming to the United States and their ongoing stress adjusting to local schools. This program also benefited from a marketing partnership with a national nonprofit, The Hispanic Heritage Foundation, and its CEO **Antonio Tijerino,** who was at that time an Imagination Stage board member (see Figure 4.1);
- ***10 Seconds*** is another one-act touring play for teen students that reflects trauma around police-community youth relationships and provides post-play student discussion and activities; and
- **Voices Beyond Bars** brings trained facilitators to juvenile incarceration facilities to encourage youth to share experiences and feelings through poetry, prose and plays of incarcerated youth which are then shared with an audience.

> *The Imagination Stage model for problem solving is a model that thinks outside the box about how to address the needs of our children. An example is the Oyéme! program that supports unaccompanied children from Central America in our community. I was part of the coalition that was built around that program which will outlast all of us in many ways, both in the actual program and in the process that we followed. Oyéme! laid such a strong foundation that it has now been expanded to address other very difficult and challenging problems facing our youth today around criminal justice reform, around better connections with law enforcement, and our first responders. It is a model that has real staying power and one that provides me hope that we will be able to address other challenges in the future.*
>
> — The Honorable Gabe Abornoz, council member, Montgomery County, Maryland, 2019–present

Theatre for Change programs were funded by an array of sources including private foundations, individual philanthropy, government grants and subsidies from Imagination Stage operating funds. Partnerships, like those cultivated for Theatre for Change, often result in funding that would not have been available for Imagination Stage's standard programs (Figure 4.1).

In every instance, the community partnership was mutually beneficial to the government and to Imagination Stage. Mutual goals of supporting children in the community were achieved and expanded as a result of the collaboration. But building this trust takes work. Imagination Stage worked for years to achieve the respect and trust of the government departments so that when the time came for this major initiative, everyone was ready to be involved.

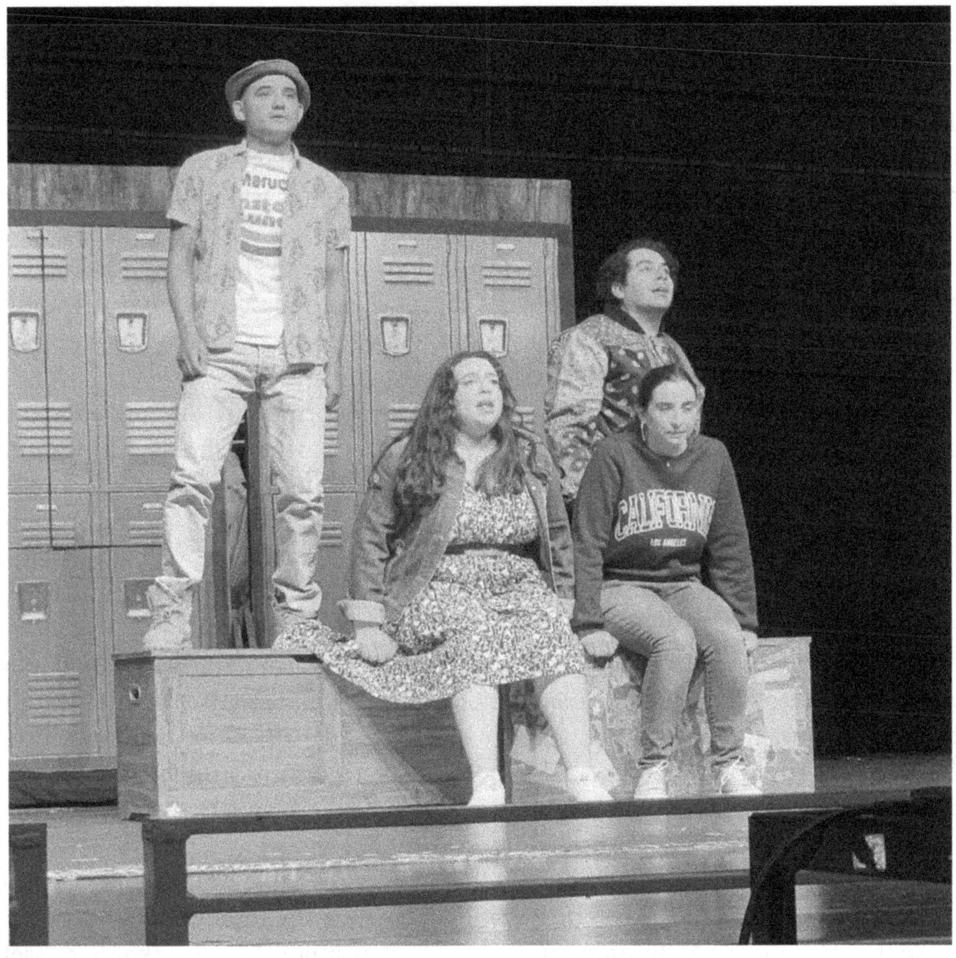

FIGURE 4.1: A scene in *Oyéme!*, 2016. Photo courtesy of Imagination Stage.

CORPORATE/BUSINESS PARTNERSHIPS

Nonprofit-corporate partnership relationships (between a nonprofit and for-profit entity) are based on each contributing resource to achieve a shared goal (this could be the nonprofit doing the hands-on work and the business providing the funds). Partnerships help the nonprofit build resources and expertise and expand the reach of programs. They may also result in board members and volunteers for the project and usually involve corporate investment in the project.

Partnerships also create benefits for the corporation including building brand recognition in neighborhoods where the corporation wants to have more visibility and credibility and offers an opportunity for associates to be engaged in morale-raising projects.

One of Imagination Stage's favorite theatre nonprofit/corporate partnership models occurred in the United Kingdom a decade ago when **The (UK) National Theatre partnered with Travelex**, the world's largest retailer of foreign exchange. In its first ten years, over two million people bought tickets for just £12. The program was promoted in areas where the theatre did not traditionally sell tickets and continues at The National Theatre and Travelex has expanded its low-cost ticket program to the Royal Opera House. This program has been emulated at other venues in the United States and is a supreme example of a win/win program for nonprofits and corporations alike offering a perfect example of an entrepreneurial, Blue Ocean strategy.

Nonprofit-corporate partnerships take many forms but the key elements of any successful partnership are trust, communication, shared values and mutual respect. Imagination Stage has had partnership support from local businesses and corporations through the years; much of the support was a straight exchange of publicity for capital and operating support, but two partnerships stand out as examples of how partnerships can have a more systemic and long-term benefit.

In the early 1990s, urged by **Kate Bryer**, an Imagination Stage teaching associate, Imagination Stage determined to add a professional theatre for young audiences to its portfolio. But there was a problem: Kate insisted we could not offer **Theatre for Young Audiences** (TYA) performances on the student stage in our compromised former school building – it would be confusing to audiences: were they coming to see a student show or a professional show?

Heads were scratched. How could we find an affordable professional theatre space that would give Kate the professional presence she insisted was needed to present a credible TYA. Bonnie remembered what might be a workable model. Visiting Kansas City, MO, she had seen a TYA production by The Coterie presented in a shopping mall! Four miles away from our compromised home, the White Flint shopping center was experiencing some hard times resulting from an economic downturn. Many stores were closed. Could we convince them to let us take over a store front, just like in KC, MO?

As it turned out ... We could! After a roller coaster ride, a former women's dress store became the theatrical home for "BAPA's Imagination Stage" which resulted in a program evolution for the nonprofit. The corporate partner offered the space for free, fitted it out to accommodate our very basic needs and even included us in its full-page advertising in *The Washington Post* (Figure 4.2).

> *We moved the professional theatre to White Flint, they gave us some chairs and made some minor improvements. Fortunately, the lighting for the dress store we inherited was over an area that could function as a stage. There was one room in the back and some dressing cubicles. We started a birthday party business and realized we could double our income from this source if the cubicles were turned into another party room. One weekend, we brought in a sledge hammer and broke down the walls, painted, and turned the area into a party room! Cakes were from Krispy Kreme. As we evolved, we adapted all the time. How to create lighting and sound systems (starting with only a boombox). Using creativity and sweat-labor, we created a really good theatre in a space that sat only 75!*
>
> – Kate Bryer, Director of Theatre, 1989–present

This was a win/win partnership. Imagination Stage got the home it needed for its new venture. The new professional theatre was so successful that it informed the next evolution of the business into its "Forever Home" which included a 400-seat theatre. White Flint was delighted by the crowds that attended the theatre and drew a new population to its center resulting in a new family-friendly visibility. In later years, White Flint management remembered this venture as representing a turning point in the evolution of their Center. And, after ten years at White Flint, when we mounted a capital campaign for our Forever Home, the **White Flint owners were among the earliest and largest donors**, their experience with us was that we could be trusted to deliver and to maximize the benefits of their investment in the community. This is a perfect example of a partner transition to a major stakeholder.

Not every partnership is perfect. In 2018, a board member introduced us to **Chris Whittle,** an American entrepreneur who had made his mark as the founder of four companies in the fields of education and media. In 2015, **Whittle School & Studios** was launched as a global system of private schools with the first ones scheduled to open in Shenzhen, China, and Washington DC, in 2019.

Imagination Stage was contracted to provide services for the DC school and, later, for the school in China – and Chris Whittle intimated that the Imagination Stage arts curriculum might be used in all the schools going forward. Whittle's plan

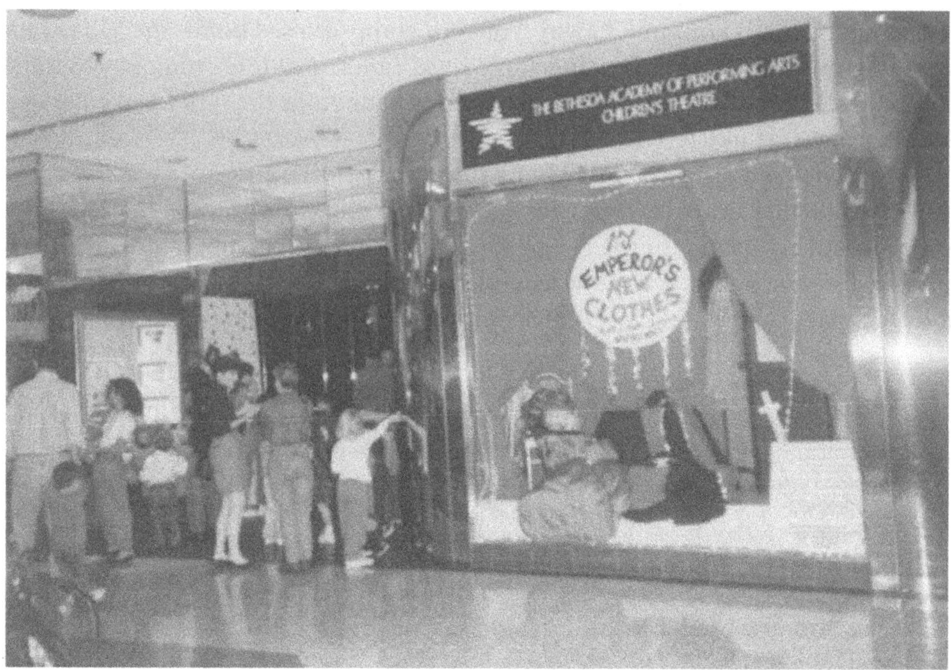

FIGURE 4.2: Photo of audiences entering Imagination Stage's White Flint Mall location, 1992. Photo courtesy of Imagination Stage.

was to establish 30 schools in sixteen countries to serve 90,000 students worldwide within the decade. The concept that students would move from campus to campus around the world (including several in Europe) was beyond exciting and many local parents were signing up thrilled by the concept of their children becoming global citizens. The confluence of the COVID-19 pandemic and other economic factors caused the DC campus to close.

As the board and leadership staff reflected on the experience, we concluded that, ultimately, we had benefited from being part of an extraordinary adventure. Spending time with Chris Whittle, piggybacking on his dream and imagining our own global superstar trajectory gave us a taste of what it would be like to operate at the highest level of achievement. Ultimately, we did not regret being part of a wild ride, regardless of the outcome. So, the message is: **dream big** and **keep your eyes wide open**.

When engaging in partnership discussions with corporations, nonprofits tend to "dream small," whether it's the amount of investment we ask for or the scope of the project. The entrepreneurial leader always dreams big, always remembers that the best opportunities may not present at the best time, and is always ready to advance toward that **Big Hairy Audacious Goal (see Trait 1)**.

PARTNERSHIPS WITH FOUNDATIONS

Private foundations are one of the primary sources of funding for nonprofit organizations. Foundations must distribute a percentage of their wealth each year and look for projects that mesh with their service mission. Mostly, relationships with nonprofits are straightforward, transactional. The nonprofit asks for support of a project, funds are given and the nonprofit reports back.

Entrepreneurial thinking takes this relationship to the next stage. All foundations have funding priorities. Some legacy foundations go beyond project and capital funding and look to solve major problems. Think of the **Bill and Melinda Gates Foundation's** mission "to create a world where every person has the opportunity to live a healthy, productive life." And they walk the talk. While the Gate's Foundation's work operates at a very high level and is mainly overseas, in most major cities there are local legacy foundations with comprehensive priorities to improve the well-being of the community who can be approached with your novel solution to a huge problem.

This has worked for us.

Working nationally. We met **Antonio Tijerino,** president and CEO of the national **Hispanic Heritage Foundation** through a board member and, excited by our arts profile, he joined the board and became a major proponent and partner in our emerging work in the area of social justice education and theatre. Specifically, he encouraged us, introduced us to resources and helped fund our *Oyéme!* project. Translated as *Hear Me!* this workshop/social justice theatre production empowers recently arrived migrant youth through the sharing of their stories. It is an example of how partnering with a large Foundation that shares your nonprofit goals can be mutually beneficial. Antonio and HHS provided credibility to our fledgling efforts in this arena by lending a nationally recognized name to our work.

Working locally. Smaller family foundation partnerships can also exponentially increase the breadth and depth of a nonprofit's work. This was true of our relationship with the **Jim and Carol Trawick Foundation.** Jim and Carol Trawick were local entrepreneurs whose highly successful for-profit business funded their eponymous Foundation, whose mission was to support local nonprofits in their county. Carol Trawick was especially interested in funding arts and education nonprofits.

Carol had a novel concept! Her **Team Up** grant called for an innovative collaborative based on the model used by their for-profit business in their successful national IT business; it required that a minimum of three nonprofit partners collaborate to serve a community project. Importantly, there had to be "lead" nonprofit and several "supporting" smaller partners. Carol's clever premise was designed to not only solve a community problem but, at the same time, teach nonprofits how to work together and learn that, together, they could accomplish more for the community than they could individually.

The foundation worked with the teams, mentoring them and aiding in their collaboration. The priority goal of the grant was service to the community, but the secondary aim was teaching nonprofits how to think strategically and work collaboratively for the public good. (This spoke to an issue where in any given community there are often several, if not many, nonprofits with the same end-point user – all using different approaches. Finding ways to collaborate serves the purpose of the funding entity and the nonprofits.)

Imagination Stage successfully bid to be one of the chosen projects early in the **Team Up** project journey. Our project brought arts opportunities to populations of students with access and inclusion needs. The partners were diverse, from Glen Echo Park Foundation, the Puppet Co and KEEN (Kids Enjoy Exercise Now). This project also included training junior and high school students as mentors for the summer camp. This program lasted three years under a $1M grant and had a major impact on the communities and on the thinking of the nonprofits involved. Key to cultivating this four-pronged partnership was constructing a logic model that delineated responsibilities, timelines, impacts and measures (see Appendix J).

PARTNERSHIPS WITH OTHER NONPROFITS

In theatres and other performing arts organizations, it is not unusual to "co-produce" productions. However, there are other artistic partnership models. For example, Imagination Stage partnered with Broadway presenting houses, the Washington Ballet and others but in ways that went far beyond the traditional shared-cost model of partnering.

In 2012, Imagination Stage won the Helen Hayes Award for Best Production for *The Lion, The Witch and the Wardrobe*, a seamless integration of ballet and theatre. We worked with the Washington Ballet to create an entirely new piece, an artistic collaboration between Janet Stanford (playwright), Septime Webre and David Palmer (choreographers), Matthew Pierce (composer) and Erik van Wyk (Set, Props and Puppet Design). The artists and both companies shared the intellectual property created through the three-year process. The partnership was unique as it required aligning multiple union contracts (AGMA and AEA) and obligations across one production in a unique format (Figure 4.3).

In 2014, Imagination Stage partnered with **The National Theatre** in Washington, DC, a historic venue managed by an out-of-town commercial booking agency, and its operations were run by the nonprofit National Theatre Foundation. The National had been dark for a significant part of the calendar year and seemed

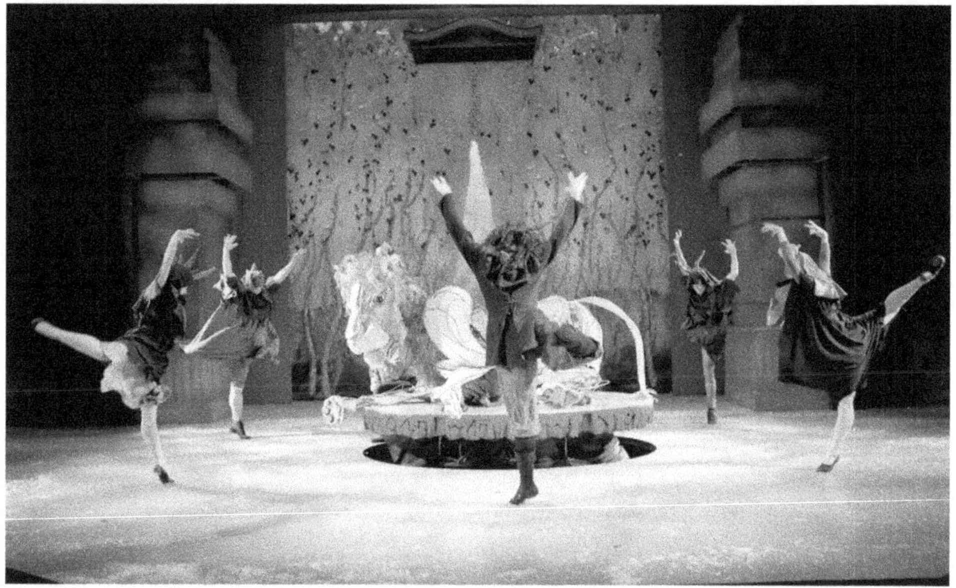

FIGURE 4.3: Aslan with the dancer-emotion-identities of the characters from the 2012 production of *Lion, The Witch, and The Wardrobe*. Photo courtesy of Imagination Stage.

to represent a fit: our mainstage shows could tour there after finishing their run in Bethesda. The National would get help populating its calendar and credit for bringing children to its well-located and excellent theatre.

It represented an opportunity for both organizations. The National Theatre wanted to work more deeply with their community and with families. It offered Imagination Stage the opportunity to serve a broad, DC-based audience. We did a trial run with *The BFG*. We served 10,000 DC-based children and their teachers for free plus families and tourists on the weekends. Artistically, we had an extraordinary experience that allowed the team to fill the space with amazing theatre. In addition, Imagination Stage was able to get the attention of major, national organizations that would otherwise not care about a suburban theatre. The partnership was short-lived, however, as the for-profit touring company began using more of the available production time in the space (Figure 4.4).

As noted above, although nonprofits may be inherently collaborative with their staff associates, board members and community, they often see other nonprofits as threats rather than opportunities. The line of thinking behind this assumption is that nonprofits are competitive for scarce resources: staff associates, board members, press, social media, customers and, most of all, programs.

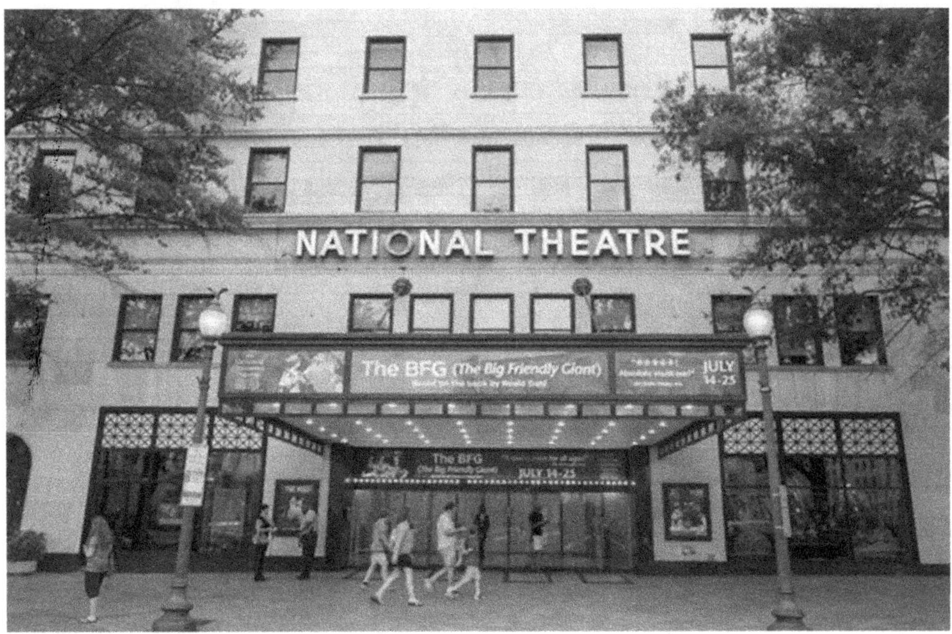

FIGURE 4.4: The National Theatre marquee in Washington, DC advertising *THE BFG*, 2015. Photo courtesy of Imagination Stage.

> *Partnership with Black Kids in Theatre*
>
> *I had been teaching at BAPA for about three years. My classes were predominantly white, but I'd occasionally have one or two black participants. A black mother approached me at the end of one of our performances and said, "This is the first time my daughter has had a positive experience with a theatre production. She's not usually cast in a visible role. It's improved her confidence." Unfortunately, children of color are frequently marginalized in predominantly white theatre environments. My own sons had experienced it. The following year, I stepped back from BAPA to pilot my own group, which I called Black Kids in Theatre. Bonnie was super enthusiastic when I told her. "That's a wonderful idea, let me know if there's anything I can do to support you."*
>
> *Black Kids in Theatre turned out to be way more successful than I anticipated. Within a year, I approached Bonnie to bring it under BAPA's umbrella. She was welcoming and enthusiastic. Bonnie understood the power of thinking out of the box, embracing change, mentoring and nurturing her staff, and keeping her love of children as her institution's core value.*
>
> — Caleen Sinnette Jennings, playwright, professor of theatre, emerita, American University

We consider this short-sighted. The best analogy we can suggest is the Shoe Store Analogy.

If there are twenty shoe stores in a shopping center, twenty times more people will visit that shopping center for shoes ... than if there is just one shoe store. Who wants a shopping center with only one shoe store?

The Wrap

Entrepreneurial traits we identified and focused on in this chapter were:

- Visionary – they identify opportunities in the nonprofit's community;
- Creative and innovative – they imagine new ways to provide new opportunities through innovative programming and services;
- Market savvy – they can "read" the market to determine if this will sell;
- Promoters/advocates – they know how to successfully promote products/services;
- "People" people – they engage the right people to help them.

Partnerships are often encouraged by funders and community leaders. This is because good partnerships can truly achieve impactful results. By combining forces, missions are expanded, audiences are expanded and new program creation might even create new Blue Ocean markets for your organization.

Often, organizations get caught up in how they have always done things or consider partnerships merely as a band-aid for cost-cutting. This is short-sighted. As demonstrated in this chapter, savvy collaborations and partnerships can be truly entrepreneurial. The best means for evaluating potential success is understanding how missions align, how existing or potential audiences will be impacted and a clear sense of the necessity of the project for the community and the organizations.

Partnerships done well are synergistic. They expand opportunities for all involved and help organizations reach more deeply and broadly across the communities they serve. They are sometimes amazing opportunities for non-arts organizations to find new value in the arts (or vice versa), offering impact and social good in ways they could not achieve on their own.

Partnerships, in so many ways, are a core entrepreneurial act as they offer pathways for the implementation of Blue Ocean visions.

Discussion Questions For Starting And Growing Entrepreneurial Leaders

- Starters:
  - Take a moment to consider how you define partnership in your current life, personal or professional.

        - How would you characterize them?
        - How do you know if they are working well?
    - Look at your competitors, especially those that are thriving, do they engage in partnerships?
        - How do they engage their partners?
- Adaptors:
    - Consider the last year of operations:
        - who were your organization's partners? Might any open Blue Oceans?
        - Are there organizations you wish you had partnered with in hindsight?
    - As you look forward to your work for the next couple of years, take five minutes and brainstorm opportunities for all forms of partnership – media, government, foundation and other nonprofits.
    - Take a moment to consider how you define partnership in your current life and practice. What type of partnership is it: artistic, administrative, marketing or all three?

Trait 5

The Power of Your Voice and Advocacy

When the world is silent, even one voice becomes powerful.

—Malala Yousafza, human rights advocate

Advocating for your vision is a core characteristic of an entrepreneur.

By definition, advocacy is "the act of supporting a cause or proposal: the act or process of advocating for something."[23] Many states have action days, like Arts Advocacy Day, where a topic is highlighted for state officials, thereby demonstrating that the arts, like all social and public goods, require active advocacy to stay at the forefront of decision-makers at the local and national level. Advocacy demands public support for, or recommendation of, a particular cause or policy, i.e., advocacy for arts inclusion in education curricula. Advocacy involves promoting the interests or cause of someone or a group of people. An advocate is a person who argues for, recommends or supports a cause or policy. Advocacy is also about helping people find their voice. In the legal system, you might even hear that someone is a defendant's advocate.

In the context of this book, advocacy refers to **educating those in positions of legislative or administrative leadership** regarding issues of importance to the furtherance of the mission of a nonprofit organization, specifically funding, and legislation. This chapter delineates advocacy tactics that position organizations for successful outcomes for critical budget and legislative outcomes. **Advocacy is a key strategy in the entrepreneurial leader's toolbox** and essential to an organization's optimal growth and development.

As an entrepreneur, you must advocate for your ideas with all the stakeholders, or potential stakeholders, in your business. Successful leaders recognize that this mindset is not something ignored while getting the business on its feet or returned to in moments of crisis, but rather an on-going process. This is especially true for individuals working for public and social good. Your work as a social good or arts entrepreneur will contribute to the public, ergo, public officials need to be constantly informed of your work, your success and your needs as you grow. In this chapter, we spotlight this previously identified entrepreneurial trait:

- **Promoters/advocates – they know how to successfully promote products/ services.**

It is rare that a nonprofit leader will have access into the inner sanctum of decision-making in their city, county or state. However, over time, your presence will be expected and, if carried out correctly, anticipated to contribute usefully to the discourse, offering perspectives otherwise forgotten or unknown. Before addressing advocacy tactics, let's address how both elected and appointed officials can and should be part of your advocacy strategy.

Elected officials are voted into office to serve by representing and furthering their constituents' needs. Similarly, a nonprofit is granted tax-exempt status because its mission and programs are driven by meeting community needs, not by financial profit. Since the service mission of elected officials and nonprofits are aligned to benefit the community, it follows that nonprofits should ensure that their elected officials know, and value, their work so that legislators will be positioned to help grow your shared community priorities. This is the stance Imagination Stage leadership has always taken.

Elected officials' staff represent an important entrée to legislators. These individuals are the people on the ground making the work happen. Often, this is the first person a nonprofit leader will be able to meet with and cultivate a relationship with. An elected official's office has many staff members, and developing relationships with all staff is important, from the chief of staff to the scheduler and legislative assistant. Staff associates usually have time to listen, to understand an issue and to advise. The legislator seeks input from them on issues. And, if you need to get in touch with an elected official in a hurry – these relationships will be key. Often, these are the individuals who remain over time as elected officials come and go.

Appointed officials are usually career professionals who are appointed by the county or state executives or the county or state legislatures to lead an agency, institution, department, office, branch, division, council, commission, board or bureau, whether unpaid or paid. An appointed department head is accountable only to the person(s) or committee who appointed them. **Heads of local agencies** (for example, police, recreation departments, health and human services departments) **can provide extraordinary support to a nonprofit.** It is wise for a nonprofit leader to know appointed officials who lead agencies that are now, or possibly will be in the future, a collaborator to their mission. Appointed officials may not control the purse strings in the way legislators do, but they *have access to public funds* and programs.

Advocacy in the twenty-first century involves many strategic tactics, all of which need to be used at one time or another. Digital advocacy has grown tremendously in the last 15–20 years, including emails, statements on a website or a social media campaign. However, phone calls, letters and in-person visits are, by far, the most impactful in terms of data tracked and respected by the system. Real people matter more than digital, auto-generated content. That isn't to say that signing a petition is meaningless, but seeing a person and hearing their story is often the tipping point for a decision-maker.

Well-run, entrepreneurial, nonprofits know that **advocacy must always be a priority** to ensure a strategically positioned organization. Regularly engaging local elected and appointed leadership is not just being polite; it's educating your stakeholders so that they are knowledgeable about your organization and, thus, primed to help when needed.

CASE STUDY: IMAGINATION STAGE ADVOCACY SUCCESS

Very few nonprofits prioritize advocacy. Many pay lip service to advocacy by inviting elected and appointed officials to opening nights and other special events, ensuring they are on their mailing lists, etc. These are the bare essentials. This was certainly the case for us at Imagination Stage in the early days when "staying alive" was the priority. In this respect, the BAPA/Imagination Stage advocacy pathway was fairly typical. As our organization grew, so did our understanding of the importance of advocacy, and our practice.

A turning point in our whole-body embrace of advocacy occurred in 1988, nine years into our story; we were renting a declassified elementary school when we heard that the abutting high school was planning to tear it down to make room for more classroom space. We and the other nonprofits sharing the space would lose our homes. Through a family connection, I met with a county council member's aide and explained our plight to her. She helped us make the case to the council that (1) the school could expand on the other side, (2) we were serving the community and (3) we were adding to the county coffers by paying rent– all of which would be lost if we were ousted. In short order, we rallied the community, got press and put on a special event where we literally formed a human chain around the building and hugged it. Media and the community flocked to The Big Hug, as well as some country council members. The result was a success! The school system backed down and we continued our tenancy. **This experience was pivotal in my understanding that even a small organization can make big waves and that every individual can raise their voice and be heard.**

Normally, we don't recommend that advocacy be seen as a tool to be used for immediate gain, rather, it should be a steady, strategic approach to educating stakeholders. At Imagination Stage, years of keeping elected officials informed about our work and benefit to the community meant that when we really needed help, perhaps a significant contribution to a capital campaign or a major facility upgrade, our elected officials knew who we were, trusted us and were willing to listen. Absent their specific and significant help, when we needed it, we would not be thriving today – in fact we might not be around at all.

As a field, arts organizations should not complain if they, like other nonprofits and public-serving organizations, are asked to tighten their belts during austere times. But we can, and must, stand united if we are singled out for cuts. This is why a strong advocacy profile for individual organizations AND for your industry group is essential, and why we must always be vigilant.

Many wonder why it is important to advocate with local, state and federal elected and appointed officials. They are unclear about its necessity or how it will help their nonprofit. For Imagination Stage, it has been critical throughout the decades.

Imagination Stage's advocacy with elected and appointed officials helped Imagination Stage with funding and legislation, and as a byproduct also provided an excellent source of pertinent advice and visibility. **It is, however, important to understand the difference between advocacy and lobbying** as nonprofits that have received a 501c3 designation are prohibited by law from engaging in political activities. Lobbying directly petitions policymakers through organized, strategic methods to sway legislative outcomes. Lobbying is often conducted by paid professionals on behalf of special interest organizations. Advocacy, in contrast, takes a more indirect approach centered on raising awareness and support in order to influence policy or opinion.

On the difference between Lobbying and Advocacy in the United States

Generally, I simplify my advice to nonprofits by saying that it is fine to advocate for issues directly related to your core mission, but it is prohibited for you to engage in otherwise unrelated partisan politics.

From the legal context, most arts organizations have a federal income tax exemption. With few exceptions, the IRS prohibits representatives of nonprofits from engaging in political activities with tax-exempt income resources. Typically, that is construed to prohibit participation in partisan political activities that have no relationship to (or only a tenuous relationship to) the mission and activities of the nonprofit organization. So, holding a fundraiser for a political candidate using resources of a nonprofit organization ordinarily is risky, unless the political figure has a prominent role with the organization's activities and the resources used are minimal. What is also prohibited is lobbying a political figure for matters unrelated to the organization's mission. So frequent meetings, phone calls, emails, etc. (normally considered to be lobbying in nature) are prohibited for issues like abortion rights, ballot access, etc. which have little to do with the organization's core mission.

In contrast to the prohibited lobbying activities summarized above, nonprofit organizations are permitted to be advocates for any issue related to their tax-exempt mission. In the case of Imagination Stage, trying to persuade legislators for budget funds, expanded space, arts district designations, etc. are certainly permissible. The techniques of persuasion for advocacy – testimony at public events, rallies, phone calls, emails, letters, advertisements, social media posts – are nearly identical to lobbying, but it is the objective of the efforts that distinguishes lobbying from advocacy. Most lobbying registration statutes make this same distinction and don't require nonprofit advocates to be registered as lobbyists.

— Robert G. Brewer Jr., attorney, Lerch, Early, & Brewer, Chtd, board president (2000–03)

Imagination Stage benefited significantly from funding and access to grants and other programming help because of relationships with elected and appointed officials. We prioritized getting on a first-name basis with leadership in the areas that could use our services. And, decades later, some of our friends from the early days are now in more senior leadership positions.

Following the successful engagement of an appointed official, growing and maintaining relationships is essential. It is like the relationship with a major donor: hard to create; essential to maintain. And much easier than building a new one. Ultimately, to be successful, we must engage all sectors of the community in an ongoing and focused manner in order to thrive.

A fledgling arts nonprofit, with immediate needs for financial resources and other help, might not have the capacity to prioritize advocacy (but they must not entirely ignore it) whereas a nonprofit with a health or human services mission must embrace advocacy immediately since they often survive on government grants.

BAPA/Imagination Stage's appreciation of the importance of political advocacy was concomitant with our growing understanding of the importance of engaging with business and civic leaders. It is all part of the same strategy. As an entrepreneurial nonprofit business leader, just like someone in the for-profit sector, you simply must "see and be seen" by the appointed and elected community officials: meeting those with the power to shape your world and your business is essential.

We have watched many new and not-so-new organizations overlook this at their peril. Similarly, we have seen new organizations immediately embrace advocacy as part of their organization's growth strategy. These latter are entrepreneurial in *all* their thinking and will thrive.

VISIBILITY: SEE AND BE SEEN

Just as your nonprofit can help bring visibility to elected and appointed officials by bringing them to your events and recognizing them, so too can they give *you* visibility. For instance, I have attended events when I have been recognized from the podium by an elected official who has been eager to show that they know the people in the room, especially if the person they pointed out has some visibility and credibility.

Elected and appointed officials may also invite you to their own meetings, town halls and events. Go to as many of them as you can. **You will always meet someone (besides the elected official) who can be helpful in your quest to find people who want to help in the community.** At an event designed to introduce a candidate to prospective supporters, you can use the occasion to also meet those capable of offering significant support to the candidate – and to you! **Those who support political candidates care about their community and will be happy to listen to you as you explain *your organization's* mission in the community.**

Take advantage of every opportunity to be visible. Attend legislative breakfasts, networking dinners orchestrated by your local chamber of commerce, anything and everything. Have a goal to meet one person at any event you attend who can be helpful to you. Do not attend and think that is all that is required. I have seen this so many times and it is a sorry sight, an event whose chief function is to provide networking opportunities and people not taking advantage of it. *You are not at the legislative breakfast to eat the bacon and eggs!* Get there early and stay late and move around meeting and greeting. Do your homework and plan what you are going to say and to whom before you get there. Elected officials are there to work. So are you! Business people at these events are practiced at networking, take a page from their book, see how they do it and do likewise – you need to be recognized as entrepreneurial – someone who knows what they want and gets things done.

I know that this can be daunting. Not everyone feels comfortable inserting themselves in groups where they know no one, walking up to someone they barely know to talk to them. Again, role playing is a great way to prepare for this. For both staff and board members.

Be entrepreneurial. Seek visibility.

ASK FOR ADVICE: IT'S AN ENTREPRENEURIAL STRATEGY

I was never embarrassed to ask for advice! It's not shameful to do so. It does not diminish you or the way people feel about you; quite the contrary, people like to be asked for advice and asking people what they think is a great way to establish a relationship – personally and professionally.

When you ask for advice, you get engagement – and that is essential in business and in your personal life. No one wants to hear someone talk about themselves, their experience, their take on all things non-stop. People would much rather you ask *them* about themselves and then segway into a brief overview of your business opportunities and challenges – and then ask them for advice. So many of Imagination Stage's huge advances have been the result of listening to board members and elected and appointed officials.

And just as you follow up with donors by telling them how you have spent their money, so you should follow up with people who give you advice and **let them know that you have heard them, you have looked into their suggestion and this is what you are doing about it** (or why you have decided not to, *at this time,* never say never!). If you engage someone in a meaningful conversation, and they give it their best consideration, you must follow up. By not doing so, you will risk giving the person the idea that it was simply idle conversation – which may then become a detriment to your relationship. I have given much advice over the years and I can testify that it is *really* annoying when people don't follow up by thanking me for it, telling me how they will be proceeding or why they are not doing so.

I also believe that having received good strategic advice from a well-placed person, it speaks to the timidity of the recipient (their non-entrepreneurial nature) if they do not follow up. Ideally, you love the idea that has been suggested, run with it and make an important friend for life.

Remember that elected officials (and in some cases appointed officials) are our major donors since they control government funds, and the old adage: **"If you want advice ask for money; if you want money ask for advice!"** holds up. So don't be proud, tell elected and appointed officials about your opportunities and especially your challenges, and ask for their advice. They just might be able to help. They have a broad perspective and can offer a unique viewpoint.

The two primary areas in which advocacy can help position elected and appointed officials are funding and legislation.

Funding: historically, 50 percent of Imagination Stage's non-earned operating income came from government grants. Similarly, government grants subsidized specific programs. Imagination Stage has benefited enormously from federal, state and county funding of our capital projects and for funds for renovation projects or grants for facility improvements. Keeping Imagination Stage's eye on threats to annual funding, or in tough times, advocating for more funding to keep us alive was always a priority.

Legislation: similarly, there have been many times when government policy issues might have derailed or complicated operations at Imagination Stage. Besides the imperative to watch for threats to annual funding, there have been many other issues where government policy decisions could have seriously affected our mission and where we had to advocate strongly:

- The time our building was going to be razed to make room for a high school expansion.
- Because of an extra snowy winter with lots of closed-school days, or because of pandemic losses, etc., legislators might consider extending school hours or shortening summer vacations, significantly and negatively affecting our summer camp programs.
- Changing a bus route such that it no longer brought children and families from the metro right to our door.

No nonprofit exists in isolation. Whatever is happening in the community affects you, so you need to keep on top of legislation to ensure you can step in and advocate for your position when necessary. There are many ways to stay on top of legislation that could affect you – all of which Imagination Stage does:

- Join the local chamber of commerce, there are lots of benefits to doing so,
- Read the local newspapers whether online or in print,
- Make sure you are on the email lists of your local government council members and executive,
- Similarly, at the state level, ensure you are on your delegate's mailing lists, and
- When you are in conversation with elected officials – make every minute count. Ask them what they are working on; ask them if they see any issues coming up in the Session that will affect you/your organization.

And, always try to advocate in the legislative arena with your peers. Many united voices are stronger than your lone voice.

WHEN AND HOW TO ENGAGE ELECTED AND APPOINTED OFFICIALS: TACTICS

Engagement must be a priority. We can never have too many friends, especially those in high places. *This takes strategic use of time and focus.*

Tactics to engage elected and appointed officials will benefit both your **funding** goals and your **legislative** goals. Your desired outcome in all your activities is to familiarize legislators and appointed officials with your organization, deeply and broadly, with the goal of their helping you with specific funding and legislative issues ... and, offering advice, perspective and visibility for you and your organization along the way.

Besides the two primary areas of funding and legislation, other reasons for advocacy and engagement include achieving visibility for yourself and your organization and getting advice. We will discuss both later in the chapter.

Engagement tactics take many forms and may be different depending on who you are seeking to engage. The approach to legislators and/or appointed officials in federal, state or county offices will need specific focused attention. They will also benefit from broad-brush initiatives.

HOW TO WORK WITH ALL LEVELS OF OFFICIALS

The following represent tactics that you, the entrepreneurial leader, will use to engage with elected and appointed officials. By adopting them you will have built a strong relationship and will be positioned to use it when you need to.

Follow standard practice when issues arise: communicate to all levels of government by writing to them about your position on an issue that affects your organization. If the issue is of great importance, there's strength in numbers, coordinate as many letters, texts, phone messages as possible from your board members, users of your product and coordinate with others in the same field. Present a united front. This was significant in 2008 when the state was threatening to cut arts funding. Nonprofit organizations, Imagination Stage included, emailed our constituents to let them know what was happening. Their voices, in combination with ours, affected change, and the original, intended cut was significantly reduced.

But entrepreneurs always go beyond the standard.

Honor and Recognize elected and appointed officials as major donors and work consistently to engage them. Recognize them. Post acknowledgments of government funding in your organization's programs and websites.

Invite them to Special Events. Be generous with your invitations. Use the many opportunities in the calendar year to invite your federal, state and county elected and appointed officials to see your work and to attend your special events. They may not be available given busy schedules and travel logistics, but they will appreciate your thinking of them and may send a staff person which is also a plus for your organization. Because Imagination Stage is a Theatre for Young Audiences, and because leaders are often parents, they usually attend with their families.

Be sure to update your guest lists continually to ensure that they represent current elected and appointed officials. This takes time and effort and is really worthwhile It is not good for a nonprofit to be seen to be sending invitations to politicians no longer in office and neglecting those who are.

Issue VIP invitations to them for your **Galas and other social events.** Gala chairs and staff often ask why we would give comp seats to elected officials, seats that could be used by "paying guests" or prospects. We understand the need to maximize income but always advise that we find ways to make it work. The ROI in the long run is significant. There is typically a 10%–15% attrition rate as a gala approaches which allows us to **"paper" with elected officials.**

- **Be strategic about which elected officials** you offer Gala seats to. We pick a number we feel we can underwrite (maybe 10% of the anticipated guest list). We create A and B lists of elected or appointed officials we would love to have at the event and make our offer first to the A list moving to B list invitees if A List guests decline or if sponsors or ticket purchasers send regrets.
- You don't have to offer elected officials two tickets. One will suffice. This is a work night for them. That said, as you get to know your VIPs, you will know who would be more likely to come if they got two seats, not one.
- **Invite board members or other major donors, the opportunity to seat an elected official at their table**, make it a benefit of sponsorship. This is a very popular move for your business donors and to your philanthropists who may feel that an elected official at their table brings additional credibility to their table.

Be Hospitable. Good hosts always make everyone feel welcome. (As a member of a grants panel that had provided funding, I was once invited to an event. No one welcomed me at any stage of the evening, or seemed to know why I was there!) Take every opportunity to engage.

At Imagination Stage, we position a host committee or staff member at the door to welcome guests as they enter the facility and we also recognize elected (but not appointed) officials from the stage noting our gratitude for their presence and their on-going support of the arts in general and our organization in particular. They really appreciate this, especially when many of their constituents are present.

Regardless of their current elected status, be respectful and be judicious, there will be some whom you should continue to invite to your special events even after they are no longer active politically. They are often local celebrities and, apart from it being the respectful thing to do, your audience will be happy to see them. Imagination Stage has always done this.

Sometimes you honor them by NOT drawing attention: know which elected officials do not want their presence announced and Do Absolutely Nothing! Let them enjoy the show with family and friends *incognito*. We have had sports stars and even a Supreme Court justice at our performances who have made it clear they did not want formal recognition from the stage. We honored that wish for them to spend some *anonymous* family time, although we were sad not to be able to spotlight their presence.

Showcase them! We added them to the entertainment – we have staged skits and cameo appearances with elected officials who enjoy the opportunity to show another aspect of their persona! We have often asked them to present awards or run the silent auction.

One year every member of the county council and the county executive were on our Gala stage singing a spoof song. The audience loved seeing the elected leadership "ham it up," and the elected leadership loved the applause. No one ever forgot the event; it was a real coup.

Another year, when we inaugurated a program to bring third graders to Imagination Stage for free performances, we created a clever video that made it look as if the new superintendent of schools was driving the school bus to get the kids to the Stage. All done to the tune: "The Wheels on the Bus go Round and Round!" The video ended with the school superintendent running up to the stage chased by a handful of kids. He then spoke from the podium inviting people to financially support the new initiative. Again, a huge success from an entertainment perspective and a good fund-raising initiative as well.

These kinds of endeavors take *chutzpah* (a definite entrepreneurial trait!). Board and staff members may be a little uncomfortable about a non-traditional approach, but it works and it is FUN. As arts people, especially Theatre people who in our case work for children, we need to always remember we should offer creativity and fun in all we do.

On rare occasions, such as a groundbreaking or the opening of our new home, **we invited all elected officials onto the stage where they stood alongside board members and former Presidents as significant announcements were made.** This made a nice "visual" for the audience and for PR purposes and, more importantly, showed the strong community support the organization had garnered adding to the organization's credibility.

On even rarer occasions you may find yourself honoring **celebrity elected officials**. Over the years, Imagination Stage has welcomed some true celebrities, including:

- Michelle, Sasha and Malia Obama (when Barack Obama was a Senator);
- President and Michelle Obama visited a student performance to see their daughters' performances;
- President George H. W. Bush, Barbara Bush and Laura Bush;
- Senator Nancy Pelosi;
- Senator Tim Kaine;
- Supreme Court Justice John Roberts.

If this happens you will also have to accommodate secret service and other security officials in whatever way they want. This is tedious and time consuming. One person on staff needs to be the point person. On the occasion that President Obama and the First Lady visited, streets on either side of the building were shut down. **These accommodations are what I call a High-Class Problem!**

Capture the Moments. Have a photographer on hand to capture the presence of VIP guests with board members, patrons, etc. Ideally, a member of the development team has made it their business to recognize these VIPs and can accompany a photographer around. At Imagination Stage Galas, a "look book" is created for the photographer which visually identifies people we want to make sure get photographed. Communicate the images widely using appropriate hashtags for maximum visibility.

Communication is the core of advocacy. **We always send information via email or letters** to all levels of government to keep them informed about our activities. They may not respond or even open the correspondence, or read brochures, but it keeps your name "top of mind." You must build your brand with them so that you are a constant presence.

SPECIFIC FEDERAL ADVOCACY AND ENGAGEMENT

Arts leadership has been traumatized by years when the National Endowment of the Arts had to fight for its very existence during non-arts-friendly administrations. **As the entrepreneurial leader of an arts nonprofit, you must help in standard ways as well with new ideas.**

Americans for the Arts used to lead an annual Arts Advocacy Day. The event would kick off with an inspiring lecture, the Nancy Hanks lecture, at the Kennedy Center followed by a day of individuals visiting their representatives to discuss the power of the arts to change lives and requesting their support for NEA funding in the annual budget. This lecture is still a highlighted activity for Americans from the Arts. Americans for the Arts would also provide materials on their website with data for anyone to use. While the 2020 pandemic and subsequent January 6 attacks put a stop to people visiting officials in large numbers, Americans for the Arts still supports arts advocacy through research and its arts advocacy action center. They provide up-to-date information and data to support anyone's visit or communication with their federal representatives.

The National Endowment for the Arts (NEA) does an excellent job of providing talking points for the visits. If you are lucky, the elected official will be present. It's an opportunity to lobby for NEA funding in the budget and to drop off your organization's PR materials. If there is a newly elected leader, try to get an appointment with your federal representative, if possible, but be happy to meet with a Chief of Staff or other office associate.

You don't have to wait for a crisis! If you have a big celebration, such as a 25-year anniversary, use it as an opportunity to visit the offices of your federal officials. At Imagination Stage, for our major Celebratory Galas, we visited our elected officials on Capitol Hill with a camera crew and asked to capture their thoughts about our organization to be shown at our Gala. This brings excitement to your event and may also ensure the presence of your Federal political leadership.

SPECIFIC STATE ADVOCACY AND ENGAGEMENT

Some states have experienced their arts funding being completely erased. In Maryland, although we don't anticipate a complete erasure of arts funding, we are always vigilant. Hard economic times in Maryland lead to tightened budgets. The former federal Arts Advocacy Day model is often replicated at the state level. For instance, Maryland **Citizens for the Arts** hosts an annual **Arts Day** during the Legislative Session in Annapolis. This gives attendees two good reasons to attend: to advocate for the arts budget line as a group AND to do some personal outreach. These annual events are critical to building engagement with elected officials so that when arts budgets are in jeopardy we are well-positioned to gain access to the legislators to protect our arts budget.

Imagination Stage prioritized attending such events. And so should you. It's a "twofer" – an occasion to advocate for support of the arts budget AND a chance to visit your delegates' offices. Legislators were often in committee meetings when we visited but that was a good time to talk to their staff. We always left materials that could be shared with the delegate – a one-sheet that spoke to the group's advocacy position and a brochure or one-sheet that spoke to our organization's status. This opportunity is especially helpful if we have a significant need, such as a capital campaign, for which we need their funding support.

While some of the standard tactics are necessary, when you are an entrepreneurial nonprofit leader, you must always be thinking about how to stand out from the crowd and make an impression! When we visited our delegates, we liked to leave a lollipop star. Fun, super cheap and memorable and connects to our Imagination Stage star brand and logo. **Be unforgettable. Life is too short to blend in!** And, when possible, *try to bring board members with you.* Board members really enjoy the opportunity and elected officials like to meet them.

SPECIFIC COUNTY ADVOCACY AND ENGAGEMENT

In Imagination Stage's home county, Montgomery, the Arts and Humanities Council annually hosts a "Pot Luck" for our elected officials on the day that the Council is debating the Arts budget.

Again, it's a great opportunity for us to "meet and greet" Council members while also networking with peers. It's an effective strategy because it ensures that the group is present for the hearing and testimony on the Arts budget. It is critical to be "in the room" when budgets are being debated. These budget hearings are often fraught with many public interest groups advocating for their funding. Arts groups must be similarly vociferous and present, especially in times when government funds are in danger of being cut. It's true that you have to be a squeaking if not howling, wheel to ensure attention.

> *One side of the entrepreneurial arts spirit is spreadsheets, thoughtful business strategies, and fundraising. But there is another, equally important: pounding the pavement, making the calls, and ducking rotten tomatoes (at least figuratively) as we did to save our building. Quick reflexes and grit brought us through unsullied.*
>
> — Nancy T. Greenspan, Imagination Stage, fifth board president, 1994–96; author

BE MINDFUL OF ELECTED OFFICIAL RESTRICTIONS ON RECEIVING GIFTS

Elected officials at all levels are advised against, or prohibited from, accepting gifts above a nominal value. Tickets to events and performances fall into this category. To circumvent this, and to not put elected officials into a compromising position:

- Imagination Stage notes that tickets to Opening Nights are free to everyone, so no compromise there.

- A sponsor invites them to join their table at a special event. The sponsor has already paid for the tickets, so no compromise there.

Remind staff and board members: whenever in the company of elected or appointed officials and whether at their venues or at theirs,

- Wear an identifying badge,
- Present simple materials (or leave behind if visiting),
- Prepare an "elevator speech." An opportunity to speak to an elected official, even if, only for 30 seconds, is not to be missed, so be sure you have something to say. Always start with "thank you for your support of the arts ___ (in our State/County/Country) AND thank you for your support of ____ (name of your organization)." Then say, "you may not be aware that we have just _______, and we would appreciate your help with ___________." And,
- Follow up with a thank you email or letter, preferably with an attachment that speaks to our cause. **Send photos** of yourself with your representative – if you were able to capture them – for their use in their own promotions.

These are all good entrepreneurial strategies designed to showcase the organization and its staff as being cognizant of the importance of the people in the room by inviting them, recognizing them, showcasing them as essential members of the team that gets all this great work done for the community. At Imagination Stage, that is how we brand ourselves as an essential community resource.

Advocating whether to **affect legislation** or the opinions of officials must be a priority for all nonprofits. The engagement tactics noted above will stand you in good stead when your advice about specific legislation can benefit the discussion.

The entrepreneurial nonprofit leader steps up to testify whenever the opportunity arises! When the opportunity presented itself, Imagination Stage advocated and/or testified on behalf of issues that affected our business directly (such as funding the arts) and issues we cared about (like arts in the schools) And we always showed up to support our group, or a peer, when testimony was given.

In most jurisdictions legislators hold annual budget hearings where your testimony can make a difference to the outcome – your voice CAN make a difference and you should make this a priority if the opportunity is provided. Apart from budget issues, there are also periodic opportunities to weigh in on legislative discussions that can seriously affect your mission and business, e.g., minimum wage discussions, street closings, school policies and procedures, parking restrictions, etc.

Occasionally there is an opportunity to testify, (either on behalf of your own organization, or, on behalf of an issue, such as funding for the arts) before the city or county council, at the state level or even at the federal level. Be sure to take advantage of an opportunity to testify. It is important to be heard and to be seen "as a player." It is an opportunity to tell your story and how the debated issue will affect your clients or programs. Remember that legislators want to represent their constituents – their people, businesses and social good enterprises. **Ultimately legislators need to hear from many people to meet their** constitutional responsibilities. And you want them to hear from you!

Note that testimony is usually kept very short: three to five minutes tops. So, it must be really effective. Covering everything you want to say can be a challenge, and you must work hard to ensure you are presenting your case AND the action you would like to see from those you are presenting to, all within the prescribed time. Going over your time negatively impacts your presentation. So, practice, practice, practice with a stopwatch, and run it by another set of ears to ensure that you are getting your point across and your words are purposeful and precise.

State advocacy. Imagination Stage testified annually in Annapolis (home of the Maryland legislature) on behalf of the arts at budget hearings as part of a consortium of arts organizations. We also testified on our own behalf when we were seeking capital funds to build or renovate. For the elected officials, listening to testimony often represents sheer drudgery. They listen to days of testimony which is completely mind-numbing. So, we learned that to make an impression we must be DIFFERENT. Among the things we have done, very effectively:

- We have invited children from our programs to present oral testimony. Delegates will listen to the most inadequate child speaker when they won't give a minute's attention to the most erudite adult.
- We have presented children from our theatre school to sing or even dance. The sheer theatricality of this – in the hearing room – always works. But it must be quickly set up and executed. We have had legislative staffers crowd into the hearing rooms when the dulcet tones of one of our students could be heard through the wall of the hearing room.
- We make sure legislators know who we are before they are asked to endorse our request by visiting them and their staff in their offices and engaging them deeply in our mission and our project.

For Imagination Stage, when I was building relationships in Annapolis with a view to achieving capital funds to build Imagination Stage's new home, I spent days trekking the halls trying to meet with the elected officials whose help we needed. Seeing members of our own local delegation was not a problem. But I also tried to connect with all the members of the committee that our project would come before, regardless of the constituency they served. They will not make your cause a priority over causes from their own legislative district, but your chances for success are multiplied if everyone knows what you are doing. I despaired of ever meeting one legislator – the chair of the committee. Hanging around in his office for hours at a time I made friends with his chief of staff – we bonded over a discussion of the importance of hats! This secured my entrée and a very productive relationship with the committee chair (and his aide) over the years. So do your homework, figure out who the important people are who approve funding for the issue you are interested in – and find a way – by hook or by crook – to meet them. This will be time well spent.

> *The biggest problem I had with Bonnie Fogel was that she was so persistent. She would get a grant one year and be right back the next with a different grant for a different problem. Bonnie never lost momentum. And she was someone that you absolutely could not say 'no' to.*
>
> — Peter Franchot, 33rd Comptroller of Maryland, 2007–23

Getting this accomplished in the prescribed three to five minutes is a challenge, but it works! As the child sings or dances, large posters and signs can be held promoting the cause.

- We provided fun materials. One nonprofit that provides field trips for children to a farm always brought a box of eggs for each member of the committee!
- We have provided out-of-hearing-room dinners, programs and opportunities to engage the legislators in the work of the organization. Once we staged a well-attended performance for invited guests at a venue near the state capitol. N.B. These can be done in partnership with a for-profit sponsor.

Local advocacy. Nonprofit organizations, as a group, and as independent organizations, get opportunities to testify at county or city council hearings too, especially at budget time. The same techniques can be used as were used in the State legislature. Because the firemen, teachers, police and every other local group are also testifying for their area of interest, and because the budget cannot support all causes, it is critical that testimony be strategic and very engaging and that its message resonates.

Again, for the Imagination Stage, a young person's testimony went far to make a connection and to manifest the importance of the arts – when other critical needs may seem to overshadow them.

When our arts organizations testify as a group, we often look for a theme that will engage the legislators. Something that will make us stand out from the crowds of supplicants. It may be a slogan and/or an icon (and we will certainly ask our group to wear the same color and to show up *en masse* so that legislators can see the strength of our numbers). We have even presented legislators with follow-up small gifts, such as plants to represent the "blooming arts industry ..." anything to make a point and keep our issue top-of-mind.

The main thing though is to show up in force and engage board members and patrons in an excellent letter/email/social media campaign and. If you don't show up in person and write letters, other critical needs will almost certainly win out in the budget wars. Legislators listen to their constituents and the loudest voice gets heard and responded to.

STAFF VS. BOARD ROLES IN ADVOCACY

There are many occasions when board members are better advocates than staff associates. Elected officials see board members as the legal representatives with the fiduciary responsibility to the community for the organization. Because they are not paid to represent the organization (and because they invest their own funds in the organization), their advocacy may be seen as more authentic.

The Imagination Stage board member handbook lists four major priorities for board members: policy, planning, budget and **advocacy**.

Advocacy may be *the* primary responsibility of a person being invited to join the board. Having strong ties to elected and/or appointed officials is a huge resource for a nonprofit. If, for instance, a board member represents a distinct sector of the community served by the legislator – that board member's advocacy will carry great weight.

Advocacy is especially important in the arts. Unfortunately, many elected and/or appointed officials continue to see the arts as a fringe benefit available (or important) only to the most well-resourced in their community. So, for example, if they hear from a board member who represents a strong connection with a specific, say Latino community, and if that board member shares just how valuable the work of the organization is to their community and why they support it, that will make a significant difference to how seriously legislators view your work.

Again, this is an important aspect of board governance, to ensure that each one of your board members is deployed to their fullest capability to support any/all aspects of your work. This will not only help you make your case but also it will help engage the board member who wants to make a difference in the community.

Through the years, Imagination Stage board members have:

- **Represented both sides of the political spectrum.** Governance strategies must always include ensuring Republicans and Democrats on your board who can advocate for leadership. Imagination Stage has benefited significantly (at all levels of government) from this strategic approach through several changes in administration. For example, during a radio broadcast discussion, both **John Kane** (head of the Maryland Republican Party) and Democratic leader **Terry Lierman** pledged their support to Imagination Stage.

- **Joined staff at Arts Days at the federal, state and local levels:** it may be hard to find a board member with a day to spare to attend – but, try! Some of our most productive advocacy days have occurred when board members joined us. And attending board members will enjoy a fabulous day. Roaming the halls of a state legislature, meeting face-to-face with their representatives is fascinating and something very few people have the opportunity to do. At the end of the day, board members will know their time was well spent. And it is also a great time for bonding with staff.
- **Provided testimony**: when board members testify to elected officials on behalf of your organization, they get the attention of the legislators in a way staff cannot, regardless of how good you or your staff are at testifying. Because the board members REALLY represent the community the legislators serve. It is, therefore, an important way to get the attention of the legislators and to give your board members an opportunity to make a difference on behalf of the community and your mission. Importantly, board members can also help support elected officials in ways that staff cannot. For instance, the Hatch Act prohibits staff from advertising their political allegiances. But board members can show their support and should!
- **Provided financial support to elected officials:** a consuming reality for all elected officials is getting re-elected. Board members can help by providing financial support and tangible evidence of their support via bumper stickers and yard signs. Most staff who work for nonprofits are not in a position to make significant contributions to elected officials. Nor can they be seen to be providing visible means of endorsement, such as lawn signs due to the Hatch Act of 1939, an act to prevent pernicious political activities. A staff member who wishes to make a personal financial contribution must never, ever claim this as a business expense. We cannot overtly support those elected officials or those running for office, but we can be strategic and provide visibility.
- **Communicated with elected officials whenever they had the opportunity to do so:**
    - o Introduced themselves to legislators who attended our special events and thanked them for their support.
    - o Identified themselves as an Imagination Stage board member, when meeting their representatives in places other than Imagination Stage. And, if they have another sentence they can squeeze in, saying what the highlight

or challenge is that our organization is currently facing. This is not second nature to most board members so "role playing" at a board meeting can be helpful! Similarly, it is a good idea to give board members a laminated index card that states the nonprofit's purpose, mission, practice so that they always have it to hand!

Throughout Imagination Stage's history, the organization received support (legislative and financial) from all branches of government. This was more easily achieved because of strategic positioning by the board and staff over time.

Examples of success in advocacy at the Imagination Stage

- Nine years of **federal** funding ensured our programs for children with access and inclusion flourished and expanded.
- At the **state** level, inclusion in the state-assisted education institutes program assured subsidized support for field trips for fifteen years.
- At the **county** level, an unusual public-private nonprofit partnership resulted in the embedding of Imagination Stage's home in a 600-car county garage. This was the result of the excellent relationship we had built with county leadership over the years. And, because we were in a county garage, and therefore considered a county asset, the county government agreed to help with capital funds to build the facility and later to pay our utility costs, again, a result of building trust through the years.
- During the pandemic, emergency funding from **all levels of government** helped assure the survival of the organization.

You never know when you are going to need help from elected or appointed officials. Of course, we trust that our elected officials offer needed attention and advice based on the project and not upon a close relationship. That said, they are very busy people with many priorities so being able to get their attention for your project is key. At the end of the day, it's simply essential that continual engagement of elected and appointed officials is critical to the current and future well-being of your nonprofit.

BE STRATEGIC

Elected officials have chosen this career path because they want to help the communities they represent. So have you. Your motivations are the same. But, at the end of the day, they have to make the difficult decision as to which priority to elevate.

This chapter has mostly focused on political advocacy in the United States. The entrepreneurial mindset to advocate to public officials should be prioritized in all countries and locations. There is also the need for advocacy broadly across the private sector, notably with civic organizations – like the local chamber of commerce, and with those businesses you might be hoping to work with. Additionally, many organizations will find alliances with public and private school systems, religious systems, museums and other arts nonprofits. The entrepreneurial nonprofit leader is always out making connections with any and all players who can be helpful to them as they grow their organization.

BE ENTREPRENEURIAL

Think about movies, or TV shows, where the protagonist uses every ploy to get the result they want. As an entrepreneurial leader, you must do the same. And, you don't have to spend a lot of money to get someone's attention. For instance, for a capital campaign appeal one year, I posed in full evening dress clinging to the side of our multi-story building. The caption read: **Stop this Woman from Jumping ... fund Imagination State's capital campaign now!** We used that to great effect at both the State and Local levels. It was eye-catching, it was fun, it was brazen ... and the kind of thing that an entrepreneur would do to get attention for a new venture. Go and do likewise!

The Wrap

The entrepreneurial trait we identified and focused on in this chapter was:

- Promoters/advocates – they know how to successfully promote products/ services.

Advocating and working with public officials should be a core activity of nonprofit work. Your organization and those working in public roles share the same goals: improving the community. Your organization offers a social good and solves a community problem. You are an asset for those serving the public, but because their roles often turn over quickly, nonprofit leaders must be persistent in keeping their impact front and center.

Advocacy is often overlooked as an entrepreneurial activity, but at its core – it is exactly that. Advocating for your vision. This creates collaborative relationships that will benefit all – in this case the social good of the community. And, as in all relationships, it only works if you commit time to cultivating the relationship and building reliability, if not also trust.

To ensure a continued entrepreneurial organizational culture, advocacy must be a habit. It is not only critical to success, but it is a strategic tactic for nonprofit entrepreneurial leaders. Much like your other critical stakeholders, they must be stewarded. Like all friendships, *this takes time and focus.* In fact, elected and appointed officials are the equivalent of major donors, treat them as such. Government grants and funding are not assured.

Don't stop at the required acknowledgments of federal, state or local funding in your organization's programs and websites. Always send thank you notes and be sure to honor officials as equal to any other significant and returning donor.

Finally, it isn't just the job of the staff and development team. Fully engage your board. They can be the best advocates for the organization. They, too, live and work where elected officials serve.

Discussion Questions For Starting And Growing Entrepreneurial Leaders

- Starters:
  - Advocacy is personal and professional. What do you support or advocate for in your personal life?
  - What tactics and forms of advocacy do you practice?
  - Take a moment and identify your current elected and appointed public officials in your local, state and federal offices.
    - How might you find connections with what you are doing?
  - Looking at your neighborhood or immediate community, what issues need to be addressed?
    - Using this chapter as a model, how might you set up a coalition or team to advocate for this issue, and with what outcome in mind?
- Adaptors:
  - Take a moment and identify your current elected and appointed public officials in your local, state and federal offices.
    - How do you engage with them as an organization and/or a leader?
    - Have you invited any of them to a program just to have them there?
    - Create an inventory or spreadsheet of what you currently do with respect to advocacy aligned with the tactics provided in this chapter.
  - What is happening in your community that your organization should be engaged with because of your mission?
    - If you were to set up a staff + board advocacy committee, who would you want on it and why?

Trait 6

The Entrepreneurial Balance: Risk vs. Opportunity

Life doesn't always present you with the perfect opportunity at the perfect time. Opportunities come when you least expect them, or when you're not ready for them. Rarely are opportunities presented to you in the perfect way, in a nice little box with a yellow bow on top. Opportunities, the good ones, they're messy and confusing and hard to recognize. They're risky. They challenge you.

— Susan Wojcicki, former CEO of YouTube

The biggest risk is not taking any risk [...] In a world that is changing really quickly, the only strategy that is guaranteed to fail is not taking risks.

— Mark Zuckerberg, CEO Meta formerly known as Facebook

It has been said that getting out of bed every morning has its own risk. And, while that may be true, the risks and opportunities we focus on in this chapter are often the building blocks or key cornerstones of what become transformational moments for an organization.

Opportunities that are transformational are quintessential Blue Oceans – they create new markets that no one considered before. At Imagination Stage, in our later management years, we would say that the big risks were akin to Apple creating the iPad. It hadn't existed before and no one knew they needed it. But, clearly touch tablets and screens *were* exactly what we needed and a new market was born.

Every opportunity is rife with risk, and the entrepreneur carefully considers the circumstances and then steps forward with courage. For Apple, the iPad was a huge risk, but Apple has a structure and financial framework that allows for long-term research and development. Most nonprofits do not. It takes evaluating opportunities against a backdrop of potential risks to determine both whether the risk is worth it and, more so, how you can mitigate the identified risks as you move forward. But, as *Who Moved My Cheese*,[24] the book by Spencer Johnson so aptly demonstrated, if you don't take risks and adapt to a changing world – you will be out of business.

In this chapter, we will unpack the need for taking opportunities and how to manage the associated risks. This chapter will address the entrepreneurial traits:

- Market savvy – they can "read" the market to determine if this will sell;
- Effective risk managers – they have the administrative capabilities to manage innovation and financial and reputational risk.

Risk is a mindset – failure is a lesson, not a stop. Learning, adapting and trying again is what makes an entrepreneurial practice.

- The world is full of examples of visionary **for-profit entrepreneurs** who take extreme risks with new initiatives that do not work out. These entrepreneurs are usually heavily capitalized and can afford to do the unthinkable with the clear understanding that if it doesn't work – they won't go under.
- Not so the nonprofit entrepreneur. While for-profit tech moguls can try and fail big when they attempt the Big Hairy Audacious Goals espoused by Jim Collins and Jerry Porras in their book *Built to Last: Successful Habits of Visionary Companies*,[25] the nonprofit is almost always under-capitalized and must understand **the delicate balance between risk and opportunity**, tread carefully, have an exit plan and do not risk all.

The entrepreneurial nonprofit leader regularly sets time aside to reflect on how to ensure that their business not only survives but thrives. Since the essence of a nonprofit business is that it serves its community, it is especially important that it adapts as the community changes. It is essential to represent the ever-changing community nonprofits served while not allowing "the tail to wag the dog," i.e., going off in a new direction (perhaps one that offers a new funding source) but that does not represent the **foundational vision** of the organization.

There *are* examples of nonprofits who *changed* their foundational vision, especially in the health and human services sector where, for example, some charities were established to fund a deadly illness that has since been eradicated, these charities have built successful funding organizations and have successfully pivoted to fund new illnesses. (The March of Dimes was established in 1938 to fight polio, when their work led to its eradication in the United States, the organization expanded its mission to address healthy pregnancies.) Generally speaking, the founding mission of a nonprofit should not warp over time. Successful organizations brand themselves with their founding vision and are identified as such by their community.

Reflection time of the entrepreneurial nonprofit leader may consider expanding in the following ways:

- to a geographical area not currently served;
- to a population not currently served;
- with a new program or service that expands opportunities for community engagement.

Imagination Stage has always built time for reflection into the leadership calendar and has expanded in all the ways listed above.

SWOT System

There are many tools available to managers for evaluating a business opportunity. Assumed in this reflection is ensuring that the project is highly aligned with the mission and has some financial return, be it through contributed or earned income. We recommend, however, that after that evaluation the entrepreneurial leader evaluates the opportunity using a SWOT. A SWOT analysis is often helpful when trying to balance risks and opportunities. As with all management tools, SWOT only takes you so far – in the end, it is up to the leader to make a decision – and with risk and opportunity that is often based on a gut feeling rather than metrics. SWOT offers a process for a strategic approach to decision-making to consider your nonprofit's (internal) Strengths and Weaknesses alongside its (external) Opportunities and Threats.[26] (see Figure 6.1)

When considering Opportunities, analyze your internal strengths and weaknesses first.

What are our Strengths?

- What do we do well? What do we do best?
- What's unique about our organization?
- What does our customer base like about our organization?
- Which of our programs beat out our competition?

What are our Weaknesses?

- Which programs are underperforming and why?
- How do we rank against our competitors?

Then ask: What does our community need that we might offer? What are our Strengths in this area? And, therefore, what are our Opportunities?

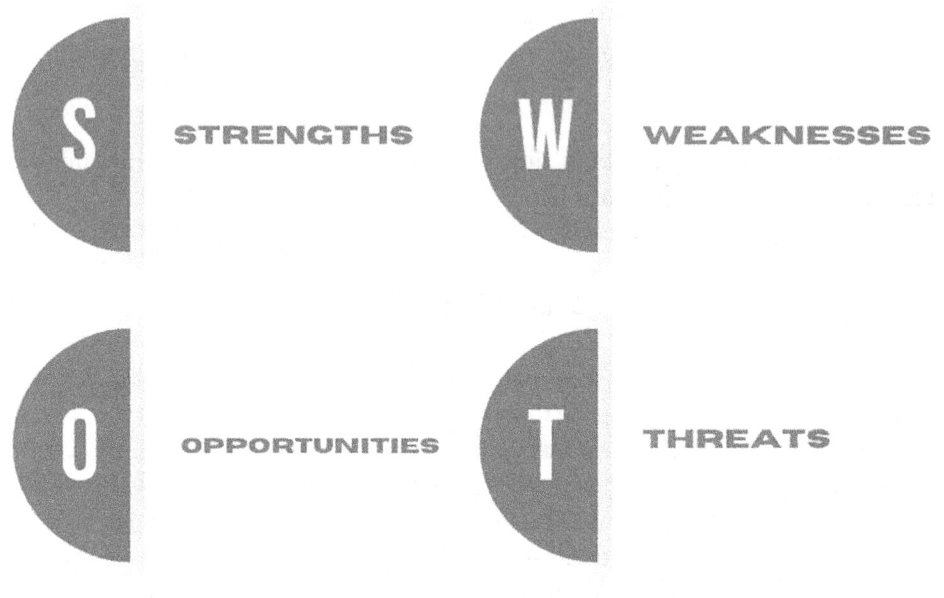

FIGURE 6.1: A SWOT Matrix. Image by Samantha Sonnet.

And, critically, what are the Threats (risks) ... what external conditions could cause problems as we consider this initiative. What changes in our nonprofit field are cause for concern?

- What new market trends are on the horizon?
- Where are our competitors outperforming us?
- Do we have the capacity (human and financial resources) to consider this?

Embracing SWOT as a habit will, in turn, make using this framework for larger ventures to meet emerging needs less scary. It's just a habit of mind to recognize where you're strong, where you aren't and what is out in the world that the organization can do and against what forces.

> *Many arts organizations have been so frightened by fiscal issues that they have stopped taking risks. They become too conservative in their art-making. They create works that are like other works that sold well in the past. And they start each project with the words, "How much can we spend?"*
>
> — Michael M. Kaiser, *Curtains?: The Future of the Arts in America,* chairman, DeVos Institute of Arts Management, University of Maryland

CASE STUDY: IMAGINATION STAGE ENTREPRENEURIAL LEADERSHIP MEANS OPPORTUNITY AND REQUIRES RISK

At Imagination Stage we took a lot of risks understanding that **risk is the other side of the opportunity coin. Risks can be financial, reputational or cultural – and maybe all three.** However, risks are essential if your organization is going to survive. Organizations that do not risk, do not grow. As President Jimmy Carter used to quote his high school teacher Julia Coleman: "We must adjust to changing times and still hold to unchanging principles." Thus, an institution's mission, vision and values often stay the same while their operations and programs adapt.

At Imagination Stage, we were early adopters of the entrepreneurial model. Some of this was the result of my first career working in retail for Marks & Spencer (M&S). At the time, M&S was the UK's leading High Street retailer and heralded as an innovative, forward-thinking organization. Although M&S was a profit-making enterprise, the lessons learned there apply to any organization:

- Develop a reputation for **quality products** that represent value: excellent sales and customer loyalty will follow.
- Adopt "**the customer is always right**" approach which translates into happily taking back a pair of year-old pajamas if the customer felt they hadn't lasted as long as they should(!). This approach leads to solid sales and breeds a loyal customer base.
- Provide **generous employee benefits** that promote the health and welfare of associates. (M&S did this long before it became the standard practice of a good business, it built a staff with absolute loyalty to the firm, helped build long-term staff associates and branded the organization in the community as a business you wanted to support with your patronage.) The happy staff promotes good customer–staff relationships.
- Nurture **partnerships** with manufacturers to ensure a quality product and solid business arrangement, leading to a sales edge over other high school retailers who did not have the same quality control culture.

- **Practice excellent community support:** philanthropic involvement with the community ensured the further establishment of a known brand that represented excellence, value and community involvement. (Nonprofits are not in a position to be financially philanthropic but can support others in the community in many other ways.)

Interestingly M&S – in those days – spent no money on advertising, believing that a happy customer was the only advertising you needed. Notably, in arts and culture, most audiences come from word-of-mouth. At one time, M&S led the retail world in sales per square foot validating its belief in word-of-mouth advertising. That approach held for about 40 years. M&S was founded in 1884 and continues to operate over 900 stores throughout the United Kingdom.

Like all great companies, **M&S assumed risk** – and like all companies, some worked, some didn't. The decision to expand overseas did not succeed in most countries at the time. While a separate decision to offer "fresh not frozen" foods was truly innovative when introduced in the 1960s in the United Kingdom. **For M&S, the risk associated with selling perishables, when you have formerly been known for selling clothes, was enormous.** But it worked because the community wanted a source of food that represented quality and value, in the same way, that the clothes they bought at M&S represented quality and value. The organization understood that quality and value were their brand. Their commitment to their staff, community and produce-supplying partners represented a reasonable mitigation of the risk. Significantly, this 1960s risk to expand its food sales continues to lead its strategy today, and international expansion is being revisited.

The entrepreneurial leader sees opportunities everywhere. They perhaps see too many! Thus, a strategic approach is critical to minimize becoming scrambled and "going off" in every direction with every new opportunity. Getting your best ideas in the shower is not a strategic approach. However, inspiration requires time to think expansively about and assess new opportunities, perhaps arising from:

- External changes in the community (new developments, school system changes, etc.
- Internal changes, is there someone(s) on staff who has talent that has not been maximized; have staff been talking about new things they would like to do?
- Your organization's capacity to expand.
- Your organization's need to find a new earned income line.

One of our most successful board members touted taking time as one of his best practices. He was a very busy executive, but Friday afternoons were set aside for "thinking." He considered having time and space to focus on random thoughts, and maybe a list of ideas he had jotted down during the week with the intention of thinking about at this strategic time.

At Imagination Stage, before the upcoming year's budget was finalized, **Artistic Director Janet Stanford** and I adopted a practice whereby we scheduled a relaxing evening together over dinner and drinks to share ideas we each were thinking about that might work for the organization and the ever-expanding community we served. Sometimes, we shared random ideas, often we just "brain bashed" about the community, its needs and our capacity to answer them. If anything rose to the top; we followed up with a get-together with other leadership staff and board to share our ideas and get their thoughts.

This process of "putting it out there" *might* lead to a eureka shower moment, it *would definitely* lead to a process where new ideas were "top of mind." With all new opportunities, no matter how exciting, first and last, we always needed to ask: does this new venture support our mission?

Having established that a new opportunity supported the mission and practices of Imagination Stage, it was critical to the success of the new project to determine who would be the point person. **Even world changing ideas and programs can only be successful if someone on staff (other than leadership) is passionate about making it happen.** Ideally, someone on the board also shares that passion. Your staff project leader is someone with a passion for the project who will work from sun-up to sun-down and into the night if necessary to make it happen.

After the decision was made, the new programs would be manifested in our **strategic management dashboard** (see Appendix G) with appropriate metrics, goals and responsibilities. The dashboard covered the core three Ws – **who** is doing **what, when.** This accountability matrix focuses on the work of the staff and board. At Imagination Stage, the dashboard was used by staff and shared with board members for their approval and support and tracked throughout the year.

At Imagination Stage, as we grew, **significant risks were taken as new opportunities surfaced.** In each case, the board and staff carefully considered the pros and cons before moving forward. Sometimes the board and staff disagreed! Like M&S expanding into chilled foods, some of our risks represented an adjustment to changing times, but the organizational culture of nourishing a child's creative spirit with a view to preparing them to embrace the complexity of their world was always uppermost in our minds as we wrestled with **balancing opportunities and risks.**

Looking back at the history of Imagination Stage over four decades, four **major risks and opportunities resulted in significant organizational evolution.** Each venture represented risk; each resulted in seismic change that, when compounded year-over-year, caused our fledgling business created by two moms to transition from its community grassroots origins into one of the nation's largest arts education and theatre institutions. This is why Imagination Stage won *Inc* magazine's coveted Award for *fastest growing company* in 2003. **None of this would have happened without an entrepreneurial and strategic approach that diligently and regularly sought opportunities that reflected the organization's mission and included analysis of data and financials that could be supported.**

At Imagination Stage, all four of these major **opportunities/ risks were financial, reputational and cultural** and over time they came to represent Blue Ocean evolutions of the business beyond its then-current portfolio of programs and markets. In each instance, one person was primarily responsible for having the passion and determination to ensure the success of the program, and, critically, one or more board members helped lead the charge and the change.

As noted in Trait 1: "The Vision Thing," in 1989 Bethesda Academy of Performing Arts initiated programming to serve children with **access and inclusion** needs. Our plan was to hire the inspirational **Sally Bailey** to head the program. In 1989, we were ten years old, barely sustainable and committing to this financial outlay represented a significant **financial, reputational and cultural risk;**

- **The financial risk:** we were committing very scarce resources to a new program with funds we did not have.
- The **reputational risk:** it would be terrible if we failed to serve this community well or even adequately.
- The **cultural risk:** some of our parents were concerned that this new programming might negatively impact their own neurotypical children's experience.

It was an intense time. Some board members refused to vote for the new programming. Thanks to the advocacy of one board member, the majority of the board voted to support the program. We overcame the opposition, plowed ahead, found the money and went on to produce the **Arts Access Program**, the nation's first program to offer theatre programs to children with access and inclusion needs. **This stands as an excellent example of how the board can help mitigate organizational issues in partnership with leadership.**

A word here about the **rewards** that follow a risk that works. In the case of the establishment of the access and inclusion programming at Imagination Stage, the rewards were immediate **and** long term. For example:

- This program soared because of the staff commitment but also because of board leadership. One board member in particular, **Barbara "Bobbie" J. Gottschalk,** was a passionate advocate for the program. At that time, a social worker at JSSA, the health and social wellness agency, Bobbie lived and breathed a commitment to those in need of life-affirming care. Bobbie became president of the board and, in her spare time (!), co-founded Seeds of Peace, an international leadership development organization committed to transforming legacies of conflict into courage to lead change. Bobbie's passion for youth development led to the **board support** needed to ensure the program's success.

- Very soon after launching the program, Sally brought to our attention that it did not serve the children who were Deaf, the Children of Deaf Adults (CODA) or hard of hearing. Again, the answer presented itself when our dance faculty member **Lisa Agogliati** offered to learn sign language so that she could support a young woman who wanted to participate in a summer camp program. Buoyed by the success of her program, Lisa worked with Sally to establish the **Deaf Access Program.** Together, these programs came to define the Imagination Stage philosophy and practice of Inclusion and Access and led to **organizational cultural change.** Lisa dedicated herself to this program for over a decade and became a national authority on integrating theatre into the lives of children who are Deaf, hard of hearing or CODA.

> *Being Deaf myself from a Deaf family, I missed out on so much as a child. There were no Deaf children during my time. I discovered the arts and my love for the arts when I attended Gallaudet University. I have always known how valuable the arts are for any child, especially for Deaf children. Many parents (Deaf and hearing) of Deaf children always expressed their gratitude that there was a program for their children. The grant from the Department of Education allowed Lisa and me to expand the Deaf Access Program. Because of this we recognized that the program for the Deaf Community was invaluable.*
>
> — Donna Salamoff, Imagination Stage associate director, Deaf Access Program, 1994–2005; director Santa Fe School for the Deaf Theatre Program

Another **long-term reward** was the way the program helped our students shine. One of my favorite examples of that period is of our student **J.P. Illaramendi.** J.P. used to say his initials stood for "Just Perfect." J.P. personified our belief that cognitive differences need not define a young person. J.P.'s verbal issues did not get in the way of his fine sense of comedy. He proved himself in his student performances and Janet cast him in two of her professional productions where his lack of verbal dexterity would not be an issue. J.P. was also a fine artist and one of his pieces is hung at Imagination Stage. Perhaps his finest moments occurred when he accompanied me to County and State to provide testimony to legislators on behalf of Imagination Stage and our need for capital funding. He was always a hit with his comic sense of timing and his authentic delivery.

Long-term rewards create institutional shifts, including the fact that today, access and inclusion are a philosophy and practice at Imagination Stage, as opposed to simply a program offering for a discrete population.

As noted in Trait 1, in 1992 Imagination Stage expanded programming to include **Professional Theatre for Young Audiences.** The opportunity to expand from our student performances to professional theatre productions for young audiences was huge and intriguing. It was further unique to the community as we opened the first theatre on the East Coast in a shopping mall. Leadership staff and the board were excited. That said, such a move represented a **significant financial, reputational and cultural risk.**

- The **financial risk:** we did not fully comprehend how this decision might completely change our business model and the risk that would be inherent in that.
- The **reputational risk:** our personal and professional reputations in the theatre community might be damaged if we failed to deliver a good product.
- The **cultural risk:** we were changing our "educational brand" – would this be seen as complementary to our classes, student performances and summer programming, or would it be seen as in opposition to our traditional work as educators.

Board and staff were excited by this opportunity; this expansion represented an opportunity to provide children and families with superb theatre for young audiences and would complement our theatre education teaching by providing an example of excellent theatre. From the beginning, we wanted to present theatre that educated while it entertained: deep, meaningful work with a quality aesthetic. We yearned for this opportunity, it appealed to our artistic souls.

Business discussions focused on how we would balance the new expenses with new earned income, with new sources of contributed income and that there would be cross-marketing opportunities as increased visibility would boost education sales.

We were successful and the rewards were immediate and long-term. The opportunity had been taken; the risks had been overcome. While our first audience comprised only eleven people, by the time we left in 2003, we were seating 20,000 a year and offering classes, student performances and summer camps in the space.

The highly entrepreneurial initiative was also a great example of how a board can be engaged to ensure success. Our staff could not have done this alone. Apart from **Jerry Morenoff**, who helped negotiate the contract at the shopping mall, two other board members with business experience stepped up to ensure that the new business venture maximized income and outreach. **Gene Smith** and **J.J. Finkelstein** were invaluable. These were busy career businessmen, and yet they found time to help with the new project for several hours a week. **If your goals and aspirations are big enough, audacious enough and hairy enough, your board members will find time to help you.** We once asked Jerry Morenoff why he prioritized finding time to help us, his answer: **because it's fun!** Nonprofits offer an opportunity to board members to engage in heady activities that represent valuable community service, provide opportunities for their own creativity and, yes, offer them some fun! For staff at the new mall-based professional theatre, these board members represented a weekly sounding board as we figured out how to make this theatre financially sustainable.

The rewards also included the addition to our theatre staff an artist with an insatiable thirst to present TYA: **Janet Stanford** complemented Kate's work and went on to become Imagination Stage's Artistic Director for 30 years during which time she developed the programming that transitioned the company from a modest community arts center to a nationally significant **Theatre for Young Audiences.** In addition to commissioning dozens of plays from top national and international playwrights, she spearheaded signature Imagination Stage programming such as:

- Initiating a series of **Bio Tech** plays that used theatre to examine ethical issues surrounding biotechnology;
- Creating the **Youth Speaks to Age** series of plays that featured Hip Hop, Anime and Bollywood as a way to further engage young audiences;
- Partnering with **Washington Ballet** to produce two classics: *The Lion, the Witch and the Wardrobe* and *The Little Mermaid* to great acclaim;
- Creating a new U.S. genre of **Theatre for Very Young Audiences** (ages 1–4) that devised age-appropriate participatory theatre experiences for very young children; and
- Instigating **Social Justice Theatre** that expanded our theatre canon to create new productions that spoke to current issues.

Under Janet and Kate's leadership, Imagination Stage received 28 Helen Hayes nominations (the industry standard for excellence in the DC metropolitan area). Their superb leadership through three decades resulted in Imagination Stage's recognition as a national leader in professional theatre and arts education.

The risky decision to invest time, energy and passion into the new Imagination Stage Theatre for Young Audiences resulted in Imagination Stage evolution to a company that was seen to be primarily a professional theatre and secondly an arts education center. The new profile "set the stage" for the future and elevated Imagination Stage to a nationally recognized institution. This was the ultimate reward of a significant risk taken to meet a singular opportunity. A model entrepreneurial endeavor.

As noted in Trait 1, in 2003 the stage was now, literally, set for the **biggest risk of all** ... our decision to find a **Forever Home.** This period represented a confluence of need and opportunity. Threatened with eviction at the two venues where we provided our education and theatre programs we had to find a new home for both programs quickly.

It was at this existential moment Board Member **Gene Smith**, who had been so helpful with the establishment of Imagination Stage at the shopping mall, re-entered the picture. Smith, who was well-connected in business and government circles, heard that the County Council was looking to establish a nonprofit in the lower levels of an anticipated parking garage in Bethesda (our local urban center). He encouraged us to apply, helped us with the application and supported strategic advocacy efforts with political leadership to ensure we would get a good hearing. In fact, throughout this project, the entire board went above and beyond – giving of their wisdom, wealth and professional services.

Our application was successful. But ... be careful what you wish for. The huge lift began. The risks were many, they were **financial, reputational and cultural.**

- **Financial risk:** our eleven-person nonprofit with its budget size of $750,000 needed to lift well above our weight to make this happen. The learning curve was extremely steep. All aspects of design and construction had to be processed. At the same time, the capital funds needed were beyond anything we had ever faced. Up to this point, the nonprofit's best fund-raising year had netted $250,000. The size, dimensions and costs associated with the building went through many generations; **we ended up having to raise $13M to build and equip a 40,000 sq. ft. building.**
- **Reputational risk:** our fund-raising consultant undertook a "quiet campaign" to position us for the capital campaign. She reported that the word on the street was that **we had bitten off more than we could chew.** And this was in the early days when we thought we needed to raise between $4M and $6M. We didn't disagree! She also learned that major philanthropists in town were scoffing at the idea that we could go from a theatre that seated **20,000 audience members a season** to one that had the capacity to seat **20,000 a show**. Suffice to say, we also had our doubts, but when a board member suggested we adopt a sports business model we did so, designing "boxes" and selling them to corporations in advance of the opening, to be used for their guests. **This ensured that even if we didn't have bottoms in those seats – the seats would, at least, have been paid for!** And, a nice touch for the box-holders, we offered to seat schools in them at no cost to the school, subsidized by the corporate box-holder. Another win-win which bred good will and also ensured a fuller audience.

- **Cultural risk:** we supplemented the work of our consultant with focus groups to learn if there were other negatives we would have to overcome. We learned that people:
  - o Thought the new theatre would be too big, people liked the coziness of the mall theatre;
  - o Wouldn't drive into town, and were afraid of parking problems – even though the complex was being built into a parking garage!
  - o Thought we would have to significantly raise prices and they wouldn't be able to afford to participate;
  - o Didn't want any changes; they liked the mall location.

> *The concept [of building the theatre in the garage] was a huge success. But the real success is not so much the manifestation of the building. It is not so much that it was an economic success in the sense of creating jobs. It is a cultural success in that we have entertainment in the heart of Bethesda. Bringing the community together, ensuring that young people have the opportunity to grow, advance, and dream.*
>
> – The Honorable Isaiah "Ike" Legget, county executive of Montgomery County, 2006–18

Entrepreneurs find the right people when they pursue new opportunities. One of the **rewards** of taking on this mammoth fundraising goal was that we were able to persuade **Judi Canter**, the parent of one of our students and a first-class fundraiser, to leave her better-paying job and join us. *In lieu* of a commensurate salary we offered her: the chance to work closer to home, a four-day work week *and* **the opportunity to make a difference** by being part of a truly exciting project. She was delighted and proved to be a pivotal player in the capital campaign. I doubt we could have done as well as we did without her experience, passion for theatre and complete confidence in the project and why everyone would want to support it. She was amazing.

The negativity from potential funders and current users was upsetting. At the same time, we were deep within the project, running a capital campaign far beyond anything we had done before and tripling staff capacity. We had to prove them wrong, and we did! (Figure 6.2)

The **reward** for the risk was substantial. The positioning, proposal and roll-out of the new home for Imagination Stage represents entrepreneurial leadership facing monumental risk and opportunity. The move elevated the organization into a world-class institution practically overnight, by growing into a 42,000 sq. ft. theatre and arts education center embedded in the lower levels of a county-owned public parking garage. Staying confident and focused during these ventures is critical. A sign on Bonnie's computer during this period came from Robin Gerber,

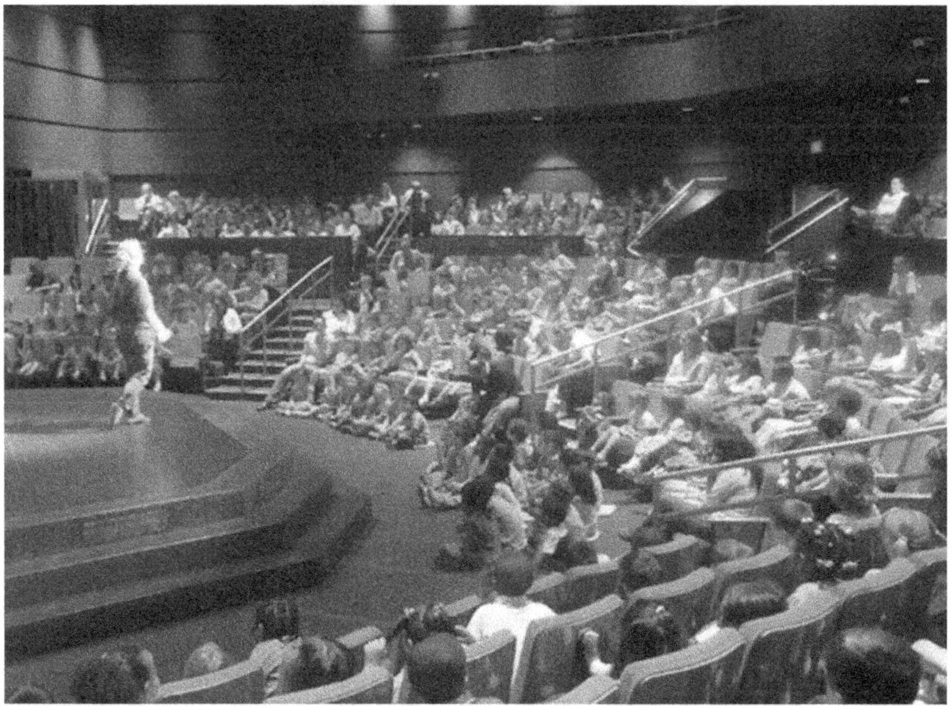

FIGURE 6.2: The audience is rapt as the stage manager begins a post-show conversation on the thrust stage in the Lerner Theatre, 2004. The stage was designed to ensure that every child was as close to the stage as possible. Photo courtesy of Imagination Stage.

board vice president and author, one of many board members who provided valuable support for the huge entrepreneurial effort: "Now is the time for absolute confidence."

The risks we hadn't considered. We had written a highly comprehensive business plan that had impressed the county and had resulted in us winning the contract to take over the space in the garage. But it was, at best, a highly educated guess as to what our actual business model would be in the new building. We did not guess incorrectly in terms of the **earned income generated – we underestimated the impact:**

- The theatre was an immediate and huge success.
- A boutique store that sold show-related and other children's gifts was hugely popular.
- The small café was similarly popular with its sandwiches named for theatre celebrities and other sought-after items.

We had created a culture that people wanted to join. The nay-sayers, who didn't want a large theatre, or a venue in a downtown area, etc., all came. We were immediately popular and worked hard to keep up with demand.

The organization had grown overnight from an annual budget of $750,000 to one with a budget of $4 million. **The challenge had been huge and terrifying and had taken a great deal of courage.** We had to navigate unknown income and expenses in the first year until our financials settled down and we had achieved the support we needed for the new endeavor. The emotional and artistic **rewards** sustained us through the change. By the end of the next decade we were reaching over 100,000 students and families every year in our theatres and 4,500 students in our classrooms.

> *As CFO, my biggest challenges were money, money, money [...] where do I start? I think for me, because I have a theatre and an accounting background, I understood both sides of the equation. That made it very difficult, understanding we needed to move forward with new creative ideas, but at the same time wondering at the end of the day if we could balance the books.*
>
> — Patricia Kratzer, director of finance, 1999–2013

As part of the capital campaign, we had "sold" everything that we could reasonably affix a plaque to! Theatre seats, theatre boxes, corridors, studios, lobby, cafe and gallery. We even offered bathroom stalls and had one taker! The main issue was that we had to take out a significant ($4 million) loan to pay for the construction costs we could not cover. The debt on the building, and the quarterly payments, was likely to prove our undoing.

Again, with the help of savvy board members who had tight relationships with County and State elected officials, we were able to make the case for several years that because we were in a county-owned garage, in which the county and state had both invested heavily, we needed their continued support to retire the construction debt. This worked for several years until another recession precluded further support. **At that crucial time, long-time philanthropist and arts maven Carol Trawick stepped up with a $2.5 million gift to finally retire the construction debt.**

Throughout this process, we learned that **the bigger the opportunity, the bigger the risk** – and the bigger the **ultimate reward.** And that nothing great will ever be achieved without seizing opportunity and working hard to overcome risk. An entrepreneurial nonprofit that has built relationships throughout its growth and development is well-positioned to ask for significant help when it is needed. In our case, county and state leadership knew our work, respected our board and our staff, and did what they could to help. The same was true of other community stakeholders, especially the philanthropists who built and continued to support the organization. Today Imagination Stage's success is theirs as much as it is ours.

As noted in Trait 1, our fourth evolution was to expand into Washington, DC. As with all the other evolutions, the creation of a new nonprofit **Imagination Stage DC** had its roots in one woman's vision. In the early 1990s, **Janet Stanford** made a presentation to a group of board leaders in a converted barn at the home of President **Nancy Greenspan.** The leadership group that was assembled was there to "Imagine" all the things we could be. [A word here about Retreats. Most well-run nonprofits have Retreats on a regular basis, a time for board and staff to come together for longer than the average board meeting. This should be a time to "brain bash," to consider all the possibilities and come up with significant new ideas and aspirations.] This meeting in a barn met the requirements and out of it came a new vision for what our envisioned professional theatre would look like.

Janet dreamed her dream, she opined that our theatre should be in Washington, DC because theatres in cities are taken more seriously than those in suburbs; the largest Theatres for Young Audiences in the United States are in major cities (Dallas, Seattle, Atlanta, Minneapolis); funding in a city should benefit from corporate presence; being in a city allows a theatre to reflect and ultimately help define the character of the community.

Many years later, with a highly successful **Theatre for Young Audiences** operating at our Forever Home, board and staff leadership determined that the timing was right to make our move into Washington, DC. We had grown increasingly concerned that although school children from DC were coming to see our productions it was a long bus ride and especially hard on elementary-age children who were our basic audience.

Again, we had the **board leadership** we needed; **Kim Greenfield Alfonso,** who had grown up in DC, was an avid arts advocate and was ready to do whatever was necessary to bring professional theatre into the city to serve the community there. She wanted kids in her city to be able to attend a **Theatre for Young Audiences** where they lived, in their city instead of taking buses up to our Forever Home in Bethesda, MD.

We were pretty sure there was an opportunity for a partnership with The National Theatre on Pennsylvania Avenue in the heart of Washington, DC three blocks from the White House. Opened in 1835, the National Theatre is the nation's oldest venue still presenting touring Broadway shows. Despite its name, it was not governmentally funded. Its schedule and productions were managed by an out-of-town commercial booking agency and its operations were run by the nonprofit National Theatre Foundation.

When we were looking for a DC home, The National Theatre was dark for a significant part of the calendar year. It seemed to represent a fit: our main-stage shows could tour to The National after finishing their run in Bethesda. The National would get help populating their calendar and credit for bringing children to its well-located and excellent theatre.

We dreamed that Imagination Stage DC would have a home where it could present its finest work and expand its mission to serve DC's children as well as DC's tourist families. Beyond that, we had a Big Hairy Audacious Goal: to create **Imagination Stage's National Children's Theatre** that would come to represent the finest TYA in the nation. And not just ours. Our plan was to bring the best TYA from around the country to Washington for the benefit of DC audiences and those in the metropolitan region. **The National Theatre board agreed to a trial run.**

The decision to move forward with this new opportunity was not lightly made and required board and staff acknowledgement of the significant **financial, reputational** and **cultural risks.**

- **Financial risk:** this was the greatest risk. Although we were successful in our Forever Home, like most nonprofits it seemed we were always one step away from insolvency. That said, we also knew that once established there would be a financial upside to our DC residency in that government, corporate, foundation and private funding would be available to our DC entity. And because staff capacity was already stretched, we needed to hire a fundraising consultancy firm to help us access the new funding sources.
- **Reputational risk:** again, our personal and professional reputations in the theatre community might be damaged if we failed to deliver an excellent product. And that would not be a simple task, we were working on a huge stage and most critically, we would be working with a union crew which proved hazardous to the health of our production team.
- **Cultural risk:** we were concerned that our mission to bring our work to children in DC who would not normally have such easy access might be misinterpreted as elitism. Again, the power of our board won out. They spoke for us and gave us the credibility we needed. As with so many examples, entrepreneurial leadership starts and ends with investing time and energy into the people who will make it happen for you.

The establishment of Imagination Stage DC 30 years after the founding of the original company felt like a step back in time. We were creating an entirely new nonprofit, at the same time we were building a new DC-centric board, finding new funders and especially meeting with the political, philanthropic and social leadership of DC. It was a mammoth effort and would not have been possible without the driving passion of **Kim Greenfield Alfonso** who accompanied me to every meeting with city council members, utility company leadership, neighborhood advisory committee representatives, the mayor's office, etc., day in and day out. Nothing was too much to ask.

When you have a **Big Hairy Audacious Goal, entrepreneurial leadership is critical as is the support of entrepreneurial board members who are not afraid to take risks and have the needed crucial resources.**

Our inaugural program had a literal BIG presence: ***The BFG*** (The Big Friendly Giant). We had created this production originally for Imagination Stage's Forever Home and it featured mammoth puppets which overwhelmed our stage. On the National Theatre's stage, they were the perfect size. We had a splendid opening with city leadership all in attendance and NT's board and ours all very happy. The show was a rave hit. The show ran for two weeks with capacity audiences.

But this part of the expansion to DC didn't work out. This huge **risk**, in terms of spent time and human capital, ended up not being the opportunity we dreamed of. The reasons were several but essentially, The National Theatre was a union house (IATSE) and that required a level of funding we couldn't sustain. And, the commercial producers determined that they did not want to give up the theatre during the time slots we wanted. Under new management, The National started to program the theatre more consistently. It was a huge disappointment at the time; in hindsight, it launched our programming in DC. Although we don't present at The National Theatre anymore we now offer theatre in other DC venues. Furthermore, our educational programs are everywhere in the city serving thousands of children with classes, summer programs and school residencies, and we are in solid partnerships and collaborations that offer innovative programming centered around social justice theatre. **The rewards have been extremely satisfying financially, reputationally and culturally.**

The four evolutionary Big Hairy Audacious Goals and the opportunities and risks that led to seismic change at Imagination Stage and resulted in the establishment of an internationally known institution did not occur in a vacuum. **Rather, they were the results of a leadership style that consistently sought opportunity and concomitant risk.** There were many lesser decisions – many of which are faced by most nonprofits on their journey. For every Big Hairy Audacious opportunity, there were **many smaller opportunities and risks** with which leadership had to grapple that worked cumulatively to commit to a direction, to cement a cultural belief and to create a culture of innovation and entrepreneurialism at Imagination Stage. The following five examples further illustrate that, like opening a savings account in a bank which compounds over time, developing and practicing an entrepreneurial approach, means that when you are ready for the big investment you have the mindset and resources to move forward with confidence.

- **1988: The Big Hug: The opportunity to save our rental home from the bulldozers.** We heard that there were plans afoot to raze the small former elementary school building we were housed in to make room for an expansion of the adjacent high school that abutted our territory. We could have "rolled over" and quietly moved on to a new church basement or other compromised location. **Instead, we fought it.** And, we used our personal resources to help us turn around the decision. We were only nine years in business at this point but we had already learned how to harness the power of the people. One friend was an aide to a County Council member and she worked to bring the Council to see the school. Our argument was: why tear down a perfectly good building that was housing a variety of nonprofits and day care – all paying rent to the County – when, without consequences, the school could be expanded in a slightly different orientation. **The risk was reputational.** As much as the community loved our work, they also wanted a bright, shining, new school. We needed to create a **win-win for both parties. We organized** press coverage by holding a **Big Hug** at which all our parents, friends and community members formed a human chain of people and children holding hands around the building. We were hugging it and showing our love. This and the ultimate support of the County Council won the day. The lesson learned was that you CAN go up against city hall if you have facts, figures and friends on your side. And a just cause. And, you must be brave. It's all part of being entrepreneurial.

- **1997: The Cutting Edge: The opportunity to add a new dimension to our work.** Our president, J.J. Finkelstein, a major player in the biotech industry, noted that the industry was having a hard time getting students to choose biotech as a career path. He wondered if we could help with a play that engaged teens. **We could, and we did.** In fact, we commissioned and produced *three* biotech plays that dealt with the issues and ethics of that then-burgeoning industry. **The opportunity** as we saw it was twofold: (1) Artistic Director Janet Stanford loved the challenge of creating what she understood to be important theatre dealing with a nascent industry and the accompanying ethical challenges, and (2) there would be an opportunity to engage with a new industry – one that was capable of financially supporting us. **The risk was primarily financial.** Underwriting was not immediate and it took time to engage the new donors. Ultimately, the initiative was extremely successful, we even made a movie of the production that was paid for by an NIH grant that was distributed universally. And our actors performed the first play in the series internationally. This could have ushered in a seismic, evolutionary shift for us but it coincided with the establishment of our Forever Home and we couldn't continue to give it the focus it needed.
- **1998: Imagination Quest: Gail Humphries** had helped us define and establish a pedagogy for our education practice at Imagination Stage to ensure a consistent "branded" approach to teaching. As we considered how we could expand our services to education, we realized that our theatre-teach-

ing pedagogy would work across academic subjects (not just to teach arts subjects) and would allow a new way to engage children in their daily class activities. Teaching at most schools was in the traditional, didactic style where a teacher talks to or reads with a class. Research has shown that this style does not work well with students who do not learn by listening or reading. In response, Gail referenced the work of Harvard Professor **Howard Gardener** who determined that some students could only be reached by non-traditional pathways and that *all* students would process instruction more successfully if it was presented using all the intelligences he had identified.[27] With our knowledge and experience we deduced that this was an **opportunity** to provide outreach classes and residencies, teaching non-arts curriculum, in elementary schools. Gail and her team worked locally and nationally, bringing our method to schools, providing training for the teachers who then went on to use the method in their own classrooms. **We called our training model IQ** for short – but *our* IQ referenced **Imagination Quest** not Intelligence Quotient.[28] The **risk for Imagination Stage was one of limited capacity** for the time and effort this took, the challenge of raising the needed funds to underwrite what the direct service fee could not cover and the availability of leadership for the project. And, happily, the multiple intelligences theory of teaching has become more commonly practiced in schools everywhere, so there was less demand for our IQ training. For Gail, the tenets and application of IQ became a life-long study and informed much of her work as a director, educator and author and culminated in her co-authorship of a book on the subject. The underlying precepts of IQ codified by Gail are *Body, Voice, Mind, Imagination.*

- **2010: Theatre for VERY Young Audiences: The opportunity to bring a new dimension to our theatre practice.** Artistic Director Janet Stanford had noted that very young children in our theatre seemed more interested in the mechanics of their up-and-down seats or the dangly earrings of the person sitting next to them than what was on the stage. Traveling in Europe Janet and Bonnie had both observed theatre for VERY young audiences that was presented in a very intimate setting, in the round, with small audiences. We wondered if this model would work in the United States.

  The **opportunity** was the stuff of dreams, a whole new community of young parents and toddlers who were desperate for engaging activities. Too young for soccer and piano lessons, these toddlers and babies needed something special in their lives. And, our hope was that once hooked on theatre, these families would stay with us and graduate to our mainstage when they were old enough not to be distracted by up-and-down seats and dangly earrings. The **risk was financial.** The model demanded a small audience of 50. And, a small audience would never cover the costs of actors, sets, puppets, props – and all the embellishments critical to maintaining toddler interest.

Board leadership was reluctant to take on this financial risk, even when it was pointed out that these toddlers and their parents would likely sign up for our parent and child classes and would be life-long theatre participants. But unfortunately, board leadership was not looking for cross-marketing opportunities or economic lost leaders. They also questioned the concept: was it even possible to engage children this young? Staff was able to secure sponsorship for the program for three years, allaying board fears and the program went forward. This was enough to get the project off the ground, running, and to establish audiences. This is also an example of the necessary tension between the board and staff and how to work toward a successful resolution.

Imagination Stage was the first theatre in the East Coast to produce **Theatre for the Very Young.** Lacking scripts, Janet and Associate Artistic Director Kate Bryer created "Wake Up Brother Bear" the impossibly adorable story of brother and sister bears who experience the year's seasons all performed up-close-and-very-engagingly to their audience. One aspect of these performances is that children are given "props" when they enter which they will use throughout the play. One of my magic moments at Imagination Stage happened the first time WUBB was performed. There was a moment when Brother Bear was trying to hibernate, but he was cold. After a few seconds, a little fellow – maybe two years – toddled up to Brother Bear with the blanket prop he had been given. Slowly all the other children followed until Brother Bear was covered with blankets and could sleep. We marveled that a child so young could display empathy and wondered if it would ever happen again. It did. At every performance, with no parental prods, a child toddled up to Brother Bear with a blanket.

Janet and Kate have written and commissioned many productions for this audience in the years since, but "Brother Bear" is still the most popular in the repertoire. And, in 2024, Theatre for Very Young Audiences at Imagination Stage still routinely sells out, leads to registrations for classes for toddlers and their parents and ensures that they will migrate to the mainstage theatre when they are ready. And, financially, the operation breaks even. (Figure 6.3)

- **2020: The Whittle School: The opportunity to go global.** One of our board members introduced us to a global entrepreneur with a view to our involvement with his innovative plans for an international school system. **The Whittle Schools and Studios** would be established in countries around the world and students would be encouraged to rotate from one to the other, thus ensuring a "global" education that would have increased relevance in the world. The concept had won international backing at a high level and the first school in America would be in a wonderful building in Washington, DC.

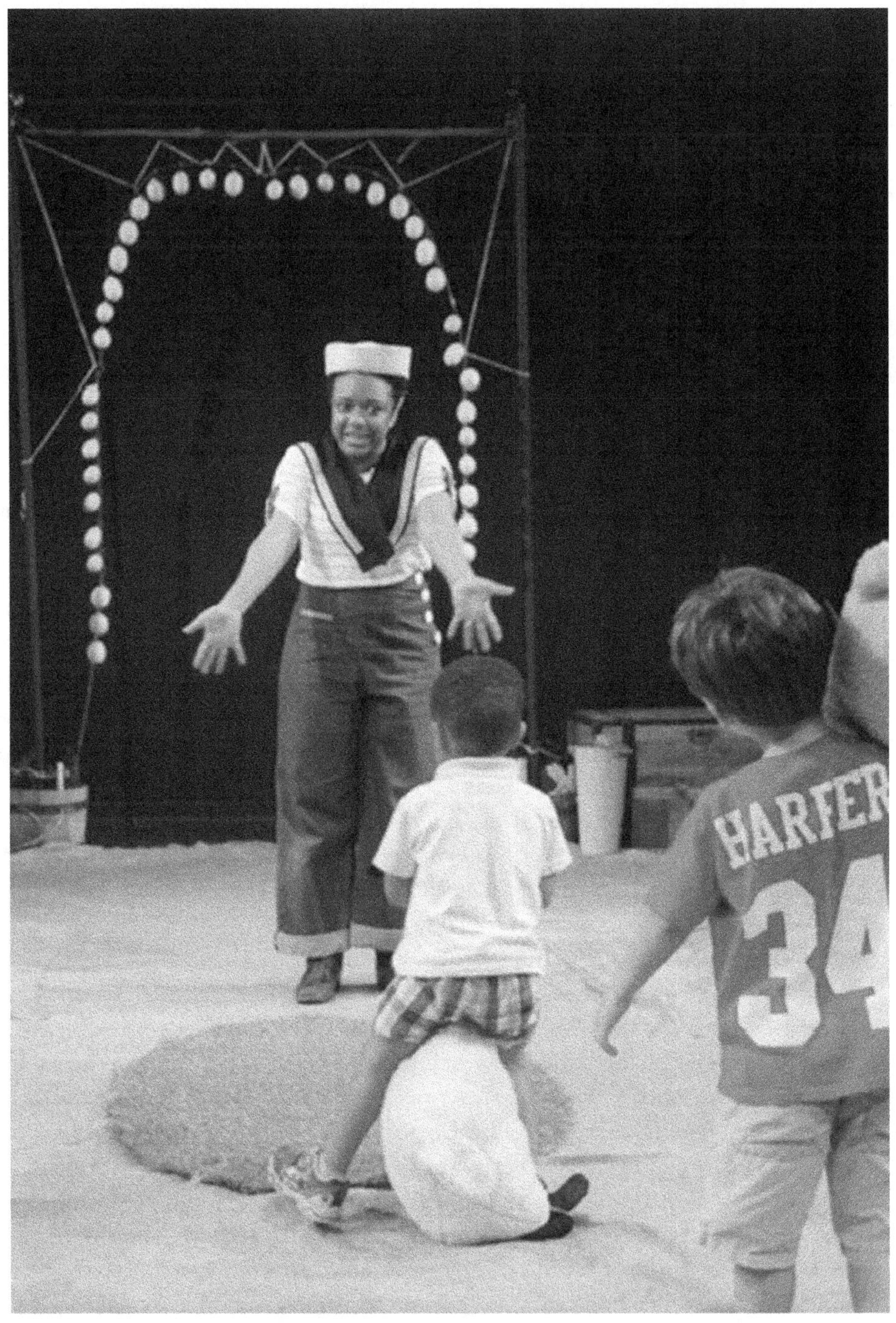

FIGURE 6.3: A scene from *Aquarium*, one of the plays in Imagination Stage's portfolio of Theatre for the VERY Young, 2011. Photo courtesy of Imagination Stage

> We were in awe of the concept and a mutual admiration was struck among our board and staff leadership and Chris Whittle and his team of educators. Imagination Stage was teed up to become an international player, with headquarters at the DC location. This would also serve as our DC home. Other area arts organizations also would be part of a collaborative there that would inform the school's curriculum and also offer classes and theatre to the community. **The risk seemed modest** in that our investment of time and talent in programming for the school would be underwritten by a generous contract. Classes and summer programs at this location would be easily underwritten by a nearby community hungering for our arts programming. **And then it all went belly-up.** The pandemic hit. Investors pulled out. The DC school had to close. Today, Whittle School and Studios continues to operate in Shenzhen and Suzhou, China. The entrepreneurial heart of Imagination Stage enjoyed a bumpy ride for a couple of years, ultimately our dream of an international future in theatre arts education did not pan out, this time, but the experience was worth the bumps.

The above examples include some initiatives that did not work out as planned. There were also many ideas, that after deep consideration were simply not pursued. Some examples above demonstrate how opportunities may fail but offer lessons to be integrated for success, for example, the Washington, DC expansion. All risks are learning opportunities. Sometimes they represented a fool-hardy premise, other times although the initiative didn't work it led to something else that did. In undertaking new projects, the entrepreneur is always at risk of overburdening staff. The leadership staff may be thrilled with the new idea and ready to commit heart, soul and financial assets to it, others on staff are in danger of becoming exasperated, especially if extra time isn't compensated. This risk of overburdening staff is real. Some of our most entrepreneurial leaders make that mistake. Tension can be ameliorated if there is goodwill and trust among staff. But too many initiatives can backfire.

Everyone needs inspiration. Even the most enterprising entrepreneurs have moments of doubt. In these times, it is useful to have support and affirmations. For years I had two affixed to my computer at Imagination Stage. One was from my World War II hero, **Winston Churchill**, who simply says: "**never, never, never, never give up.**" The other was from **Robin Gerber**, author, and Vice President of the Imagination Stage board, which said "**Now is the time for absolute confidence.**" These affirmations offered encouragement at many times. That is what the entrepreneurial leaders of new ventures and programs need. The support and inspiration of others.

In our experience, entrepreneurs will find opportunities, take risks and enjoy great rewards. And, if they do, not only will they achieve great things but, they will also have fun. Entrepreneurs are never bored.

> *You don't have to become a hero overnight, just a step at a time, finding strength, courage and confidence every time you look fear in the face. Ultimately you must do the thing you think you can't do.*
>
> — **Eleanor Roosevelt, First Lady of the United States, 1933–45**

The Wrap

Entrepreneurial traits we identified and focused on in this chapter were:

- Market savvy – they can "read" the market to determine if this will sell;
- Effective risk managers – they have the administrative capabilities to manage innovation and financial and reputational risk.

The only true risk is not to seek opportunities when they arise. A visionary will see the opportunities before others and, in that, find new markets in Blue Oceans. Risks, however, must be evaluated before moving into a new venture. These risks should be considered broadly and across all dimensions. It is rare that you can remove risk entirely, but you can mitigate risks through thoughtful strategy and tactics. Engaging in a SWOT analysis is a tool that entrepreneurs should do routinely as they encounter opportunities.

An entrepreneurial business, for-profit or nonprofit will welcome opportunities because new opportunities lead to new growth, expansion of programming reach, new ways of meeting mission. And, yes, new opportunities are always associated with risk.

Risks are multifaceted and must be evaluated in three core aspects: financial, reputational and cultural. Risks cannot be ignored, they must be mitigated. Often mitigation comes through partnerships within and/or outside the organization.

Significant opportunities will often present evolutionary moments for an organization – essentially opening up new markets and Blue Oceans. These opportunities are underscored by the vision that sees the need and the path to meet it. Blue Ocean risks, however, are more difficult to mitigate as no one has trodden the ground before. Taking time to evaluate, orient yourself and learn about the contexts of the opportunity *while* moving forward is key.

Maintaining a course rarely offers notable rewards to individuals or organizations. Taking the jump to meet opportunities, while risky, offers rewards not otherwise achievable.

Discussion Questions For Those Starting Or Growing Entrepreneurial Leadership

- Starters:
  - Have you tried something and failed?
    - What did you learn?
    - How can you make trying and learning a habit in your life and organization?
  - Do you have a set of affirmations that offer encouragement? Do they help you find courage and confidence in moments of risk? If not, ask your mentors what their affirmations are and keep an eye out for them and collect them.
  - Where do you see Blue Oceans or how will you find one?
- Adapters:
  - Opening your doors can sometimes feel like a risk. Consider the three aspects of risk: financial, reputational and cultural. What do you as a leader, individual or organization tend to avoid?
  - Have you done a SWOT analysis of your organization? Of a particular program? Do one now with radical candor, and see what you uncover about the realities of your organization's strengths and weaknesses, and the opportunities or threats that exist in your community.
  - Is your organization operating in a Red or a Blue Ocean?

Appendix A: The Origin Story

In the beginning, I felt lucky. The local school system my children Sarah and David would be a part of would do many things for them. Bethesda's Burning Tree Elementary School, located in Montgomery County, Maryland, is part of one of the finest school systems in the country. I had no doubt that Sarah and David would be superbly educated and prepared for a future where intellect, political savvy, science and technology and especially the new internet would hold sway. The one thing that made this school different from others in like areas was a splendidly diverse student body. The children of many international families attended the school due to its proximity to the scores of Embassies, international businesses and associations in Washington, DC.

But. There was something missing: the arts. There were precious few opportunities for children to sing, dance, recite poetry and perform in a school play. Visual arts classes were wheeled into the classrooms on a trolley. I realized that my children, attending one of the finest schools in the country, would not enjoy the benefits that come from the deep engagement in the arts that had made my school days in rural England foundational to my well-being and educational advancement. I knew, from personal experience, that the arts are not only vital to the health and well-being of all children but also that they offer salvation to a child who needs a non-academic pathway to succeed.

A Meeting of the Minds: Enter **Marcia Smith**! She immediately volunteered and so began an excellent partnership that worked well for the school and for the parents **... and led us on a most unexpected journey.**

I met **Marcia Smith** through a PTA project and she understood my frustration that our children were not receiving sufficient arts programming in this otherwise excellent school. She was a professional actress with a graduate degree in psychology. She too wanted her children, and others in the neighborhood, to have access to professional art education and opportunities to perform.

A Matter of Talent. As is so often the case, in business and in life, one never knows where a random comment may lead. Marcia and I were working hard on our PTA project when we heard that the school's annual student talent show would be abandoned because the teachers did not feel up to organizing it.

The rest, as they say, "is history." As we took over the talent show, we didn't realize that our work was foreshadowing the next four decades.

So, we stepped up and offered to produce it! Of the 340 children in the school, 300 wanted to be in it! We determined that everyone who wanted to be in the show, should be. (Notice how this became the philosophy for the BAPA/Imagination Stage culture.) For those children with no discernible talent(!), the producers formed groups to whom they taught musical routines, dances, skits, acrobatics ... so that everyone, eventually, *was* part of the show.

Mulling over the show, we **had an epiphany**. We realized that we were not the only parents who wanted more creative opportunities for our children. The talent show was proof that children wanted it, and parents would support it.

Maybe, we thought, we should provide that.

We were busy over the summer incorporating the new nonprofit. We press-ganged our husbands into joining us as the legal board of directors. The first classes were offered in September 1979 at a neighborhood elementary school that had closed due to declining demographics and was being used by the school system as an area office. The new enterprise was called Bethesda Academy of Performing Arts (BAPA), riffing off the famous British Royal Academy of Dramatic Arts (RADA). (*Performing* was substituted for *Dramatic* since BADA was not a great acronym!) Almost immediately BAPA became the default name.

The Founders taught the classes, did the administrative work and put the modest earned income into expenses; we did not draw salaries. BAPA was an immediate hit. The community did indeed want this. Registrations doubled each session, and after a few years the Founders determined that the fledgling organization was worthy of more investment of time and effort.

In 1981, we created a Parents' Advisory Council which soon morphed into a formal board. Board members were all parents of our students. The first Board President, Frank Allen Philpot, was director of Children's and Family Programming at PBS. His background meant that he shared our philosophy on the value of the arts for children. Together we struggled with the questions all new nonprofits face regarding the goals and mission of the organization along with marketing, profitability and sustainability.

Planning to Succeed. Frank Allen and others advised that a planning process be adopted and that strategic thinking be employed to ensure goals were set and met. One board member, **Lucy R. Waletzky**, offered that her father might be able to identify someone who could help with such a task and that her father might also underwrite the expense.

> *Many arts organizations grow out of the founder's artistic vision. They create a dance, theater, or musical company that reflects their desire to make their mark on the world. That dream can inspire people and lead to great accomplishments but many of these organizations are limited in their ability to grow and change by their founder's dream.*
>
> *No arts organization is truly the creation of one person, but Imagination Stage has been critically shaped by the work – rather than the vision – of Bonnie Fogel. She allowed the organization to expand and grow as needs and opportunities arose. When a shopping center space became available, Imagination Stage began offering performances there; when high quality film-making equipment became available at amateur prices, they began offering classes in filmmaking; when the traditional repertoire of children's theatre had been exhausted, they commissioned new scripts to expand the world of children's theatre.*
>
> *As Imagination Stage changed, so did its board. What was initially a Parents Advisory Committee became a high-stakes fundraising organization providing a significant percentage of the annual budget. As the mission of the organization grew and the function of the board expanded, Bonnie always ensured that the organization stayed close to the local political infrastructure and she made sure that the board felt intimately involved and responsible. Her weekly newsletters to board members were outstanding examples of Board/Executive Director communication.*
>
> — Frank Allen Philpot, PhD first president, Bethesda Academy of Performing Arts, former PBS kids executive, assistant professor of marketing, George Mason University, VA

Good to her word, Lucy's father contracted **Charles Crawford** [Ed. No relation to author Brett Ashley Crawford!], a major talent in the nonprofit world whose usual remit included advising mammoth nonprofits like the Metropolitan Opera in New York City. Undaunted by his eminence, we hosted him in our newly acquired office space, the former kitchen of the elementary school, where he gamely perched on an orange crate and helped us make history.

Over the next two days, Charles Crawford supervised the writing of our very first three-year plan. The task completed, a very relieved man prepared to return to New York, but not before drafting a letter to the man who had made his visit possible. He said that our benefactor would expect to be asked to cover the cost of rolling out the plan.

Lucy's father, and Charles Crawford's sponsor, was **Laurance S. Rockefeller**[29] who not only made the first sizable philanthropic contribution to BAPA but also became our angel philanthropist for many years. His championship, and Lucy's, gave us the confidence, and the financial support, to sustain us at crucial points over the next 30 years and resulted in the growth of the organization into a national Theatre for Young Audiences and a theatre education center for millions of children. We are beholden to them for eternity as are the children who benefited from theatre education and performance opportunities.

> *The early days of the organization were exciting and filled constantly with new challenges. On any given day I could find myself delivering flyers to elementary schools, figuring out how to send bulk mail, designing brochures promoting classes and plays, picking up an instructor who did not drive, creating a database of families, and preparing budgets. No day was ever boring and every day involved a learning curve.*
>
> — Lynn J. Mattingly, original volunteer and later director of education

Appendix B: Imagination Stage Chronology

1979 – Bethesda Academy of Performing Arts (BAPA) established; seventeen children of all ages in first class. The board was composed of Founders **Bonnie Fogel** and **Marcia Smith** and their husbands.

1980 – **International Children's Chorus** created; performances included: The White House, Wolf Trap Center for the Performing Arts, The J.F. Kennedy Center for the Performing Arts. The first year the Chorus was greeted by **President Ronald Reagan.**

1981 – BAPA **Parents Advisory Council** formed.

1982 – **The Entertainers** show choir established with performances at The British Embassy. The J. F. Kennedy Center, The National Theatre, Wolf Trap Center for the Performing Arts, for corporate events and television. Created and directed by **Olga Morales** and later by **Gail Humphries.**

1984 – **Janet Stanford** joins the BAPA faculty.

1986 – Parents Advisory Council formalized into a Board and **Frank Allen Philpot** became the first president (1986–88). He put into place a strategic and comprehensive approach to management.

1986 – **Cast-a-Kid** talent agency established and directed by **Stan Brandorff** and **Terri Moller.**

1987 – **Charles Crawford** hired by BAPA parent **Lucy Waletzky's** father **Laurance S. Rockefeller** to consult with founders and board to write a long-range plan. LSR and LW became sustaining angel investors in the company.

1987 – **Lynn J. Mattingly** joined the team as a volunteer and later became director of education.

FIRST EVOLUTION

1988 – Co-founder **Marcia Smith** leaves.

- **Gail Jacobs**, second president (1988–90), raised BAPA's social profile with high-visibility events and supporters.
- International Children's Chorus established. Performed at The White House Christmas Open House for several years led by **Nancy Nuttle, Rob Kinkaid, Rickey Payton Sr.**
- **Black Kids in Theatre** established by **Caleen Sinette Jennings.**
- **Gail Humphries** stepped in as interim artistic director and brought a slew of her student talent: **Lisa Agogliati, Brenda Brody, Todd Dellinger, Gaines Bruce Hall, Tim Reagan** all played pivotal roles at BAPA/Imagination Stage.

1989 – **Sally D. Bailey**, MFA, MSW, RDT/BCT, established Arts Access Program for children with physical and/or cognitive differences.

- **Barbara "Bobbie" Gottschalk**, third president (1990–92) championed programming for young people with access and inclusion needs

1990 – **Ten-Year Anniversary Symposium:** *Today's Child; Tomorrow's Adult* with **Maurice Sendak** as keynote speaker. Produced by board member **Michael Darling.**

1991 – **Lisa Agogliati** created the Deaf Access Program which morphed into the Deaf Access Company.

SECOND EVOLUTION

1992 – **Jerome "Jerry Morenoff,"** fourth president (1992–94) used business acumen and high profile to orchestrate the unique concept of a professional theatre in a shopping center.

- **Kate Chase Bryer** established Imagination Stage, a professional **Theatre for Young Adults** at the White Flint (WF) shopping center with *The Nightingale* as the opening show. In 1993, BAPA faculty member **Janet Stanford** joined Kate at WF and became director of theatre. Despite rudimentary fit-up, the theatre enjoyed great success which led to plans for expansion.

1993 – *Wings to Fly: Bringing Theatre Arts to Students with Special Needs*, by **Sally Dorothy Bailey** published by Woodbine House chronicled the establishment of the Arts Access Program.

1994 – **Donna Salamoff** joins Deaf Access Company rising to become associate director.

1994 – **Nancy T. Greenspan,** fifth president (1994–96), used community activism skills to save the BAPA home from take-over by an adjacent high school.

1996 – **Mita M. Schaffer,** sixth president (1996–98), contributed her marketing and communications firm's skills to build visibility and re-brand BAPA as Imagination Stage.

1997 – **Bio Tech** trilogy commissioned by **Janet Stanford.** First part of the trilogy was *The Cutting Edge.*

- **Gail Humphries** launches **Imagination Quest,** an integrated arts teacher training and student learning initiative. Maryland State Department of Education awards contract to provide professional development teacher training in Maryland Schools.
- BAPA awarded Montgomery County Excellence in arts education award.

THIRD EVOLUTION

1998 – **J.J. Finkelstein,** seventh president (1998–2000) used his entrepreneurial biotech accomplishments to achieve national and international visibility for the BioTech series of plays.

Imagination Quest (IQ) was launched in regional schools.

- **U.S. Department of Education** awards the first of three, three-year $265,000 grants to the Deaf Access Program.
- Montgomery County Council Member **Betty Ann Krahnke** determined that a proposed public parking garage in downtown Bethesda, MD, would benefit from a mixed-use approach. She proposed a utilitarian building that was inviting to pedestrians. The experience at White Flint convinced board and staff leadership that Imagination Stage could be successful in a larger venue that would unite both sides of the business (theatre and education) in one location.

1999 – BAPA/Imagination Stage signed a lease with the County to embed Imagination Stage in the lower levels of the county parking structure in Bethesda, MD. Board Vice President **Gene Smith** and staff associate **Lynn Mattingly** worked to create the winning response to the County's Request for Proposal. **Wood + Zapata** engaged as an architect, **Forrester Construction** as construction and **Gensler** for interior fit-out. Artists were commissioned to produce pieces for the new building: **Heidi Lippman** (mosaic terrazzo floor), **Steven Weissman** (Bottom statue), **Mary Ann Mears** (Intermission Terrace) and **J. P. Illaramendi** (Viking portrait).

- **Deaf Access Company** led by **Lisa Agogliati** and **Donna Salamoff** performed at **Worldwide Deaf Theatre Conference.** A pivotal moment for the Company.
- **Mary Ann de Barbieri** was hired to conduct the quiet phase of the capital campaign and **Judi Canter** was hired to lead it.
- Under the Campaign Leadership of **Steve Guttman** and **Gary Abramson, Annette M. and Theodore N. Lerner** Foundation and family donated lead gift of $1M to the campaign. The families who were the owners of the White Flint shopping mall were impressed with what Imagination Stage had accomplished there. They also liked the organization's work with the Deaf community which had benefited a friend.
- **Patricia Kratzer** joined the organization as CFO. A former faculty member with an accounting background, Patricia steered us through extreme financial storms.

2000 – **Robert G. Brewer Jr.**, eighth president (2000–03), presided for three years and leant his profile as a leading county attorney to strategically transition BAPA to Imagination Stage.

- **Carol Gulley** assumed leadership of the **Arts Access Program.** *Working Wings*, an advocacy play about issues faced by the employable disabled, premiered on Capitol Hill.
- **David Markey** became director of the Education Department and stayed for thirteen years. His outstanding contribution was transitioning the education program to one of process and technique, providing students with an educational pathway that also led to long-term engagement. Another legacy contribution was his creation of a four-semester Acting Conservatory that consisted of three semesters of technique and a final production semester.

2002 – *Dreams to Sign*, by **Lisa Agogliati** and **Sally Dorothy Bailey**, published by Imagination Stage, chronicled the development of BAPA's **Deaf Access Company.**

2003 – **Sally Rosenberg**, ninth president (2003–05), championed access and inclusion programs. A consummate facilitator, she introduced us to potential business partners, donors and friends.

- **Imagination Stage opened in Bethesda.** Theatre season was inaugurated with *Junie B. Jones & a Little Monkey Business* which achieved more box office revenue than all the previous year's theatre revenue at White Flint.
- Annual budget soared from $750K to $4M exceeding projected earned and contributed revenue.
- **Barbara Bush Literary Foundation (MD)** held the premiere event at Imagination Stage attended by **George H. W., Barbara, Laura and Dorothy Bush** and other Republican luminaries in attendance, thanks to the advocacy of board member **Stephen A. Hayes.**

2004 – Founder **Bonnie Fogel** named a "Washingtonian of the Year" by *Washingtonian* magazine.

- Arts Access Program awarded $278,000 U.S. Department of Education grants to produce materials and programs to help the "employable disabled" developed in partnership with **Bridges from School to Work Program.**
- Imagination Stage received **first Helen Hayes** nomination for *Junie B. Jones & A Little Monkey Business.* A seminal moment for professional theatre. Henceforth, Helen Hayes nominations and awards were an annual occurrence.

2005 – **Stephen A. Hayes**, tenth president (2005–07) introduced Imagination Stage to national elected, philanthropic and social leadership. He was the world's best cheerleader for our cause.

2006 – **Brett Ashley Crawford** joined the Imagination Stage marketing department and became managing director.

2007 – **Wayne Hunley**, eleventh president (2007–09) used his banker's acumen and resources to mastermind long-term financial planning.

- ***Inc.*** magazine recognized Imagination Stage as one of the 5,000 fastest-growing private sector companies in the United States.

2008 – **Jim and Carol Trawick Foundation** donated $2.5M to complete the Capital Campaign.

- *Washington Business Journal* recognition for Bonnie Fogel as a top business entrepreneur.
- Imagination Stage honored as one of five organizations nationally to partner with Kids Included Together as a model institution for inclusion.

2009 – **Mark Richardson,** twelfth president (2009–11) used his experience in commercial real estate to position us for D.C. expansion.

- **Sasha and Malia Obama** registered for classes during the first year of the Obama Presidency. The President and the First Lady attended their recitals.

2010 – Imagination Stage inaugurated Theatre for Very Young Audiences (ages 1–4) in the United States with *Wake Up Brother Bear* written and directed by **Janet Stanford** and **Kate Bryer.**

2011 – **Susan Lacz,** thirteenth president (2011–13). Her company, Ridgewells, generously catered the Gala *pro bono* for ten years.

2012 – **Brett Ashley Crawford** published Imagination Stage's first companion book to *Wake Up Brother Bear.*

- The Center for Nonprofit Advancement recognized Imagination Stage for **Excellence in Nonprofit Advancement and Best Practices in Nonprofit Management.**

2013 – **Jane Fairweather,** fourteenth president (2013–15) parlayed her residential realtor status and access to county political, civic and social leadership to the great advantage of Imagination Stage.

- *The Lion, The Witch and the Wardrobe (2012),* a co-production with **Septime Webre** and the **Washington Ballet,** received two Helen Hayes Awards and represented the highest-grossing show to date.

2014 – **Imagination DC** was incorporated and we welcomed 10,000 children to DC's historic National Theatre. **In 2015,** 10,000 DC children attended to see *THE BFG,* 80% of whom had never attended a theatre performance before.

- **Joanne Seelig Lamparter** joins Imagination Stage as Director of Education and ten years later becomes the Chief Artistic Programming Officer. Joanne was the first BAPA student to become a member of the leadership team at Imagination

Stage. Under Joanne's leadership, education income and programs continued to expand. She also was responsible for the **Theatre for Change** programming.

- **Learning through Theatre** launched a free ticket initiative for third-grade students in Title I schools in Maryland supported by Maryland's State Assisted Education Initiative grant.
- **Work started on *Oyeme, the Beautiful, the*** first play in what would become the **Theatre for Change** portfolio. **Miriam Gonzalez** wrote two plays for the portfolio. Board member **Antonio Tijerino** (president and CEO of the Hispanic Heritage Foundation) played a leadership role in advancing the project as did **Luis Cardona** (county administrator of the Positive Youth Development Project, and council member **Gabe Albornoz.**

FOURTH EVOLUTION

2015 – **Kim Greenfield Alfonso,** fifteenth president (2015–17). A native Washingtonian, board member Kim was instrumental in the establishment of the Imagination Stage DC 501c3.

- **EXCEL Award for Nonprofit Leadership** for excellence in innovation, motivation, community building, inclusivity/diversity and ethical integrity.
- Three commissions and world premieres: *101 Dalmatians*, *Double Trouble* and *Blue.*

2016 – Three commissions and world premieres: *When She Had Wings*, *Jack and Phil-Slayers of Giants* and *The Little Mermaid.*

- Bonnie received Greater **Bethesda/Chevy Chase Chamber of Commerce's** most prestigious award for services to the community.
- *Oyeme, the Beautiful* first performance. Tour followed in 2017. In 2018, the play was presented on Capitol Hill sponsored by **Senator Chris Van Hollen.**

2017 – **George Little**, sixteenth president (2017–19) used his skills in communications messaging at the national level to position us for new business endeavors.

- Artistic director **Janet Stanford** received the **Harold Oakes Award** for innovation from Theatre for Young Audiences/United States.
- *Disney's Beauty and the Beast* was the highest-grossing show in iStage history.
- The State of Maryland's **Board of Public Works awarded $400K for** 20-year renovations.

- The **Inter-American Development Bank** awarded Imagination Stage with a recognizing "the most inspiring and creative initiatives" **serving the Latino-American or Caribbean** community in the region.

2018 – The student **DanceTheatre** presented in Italy, the first international student trip.

2019 – **Patrick O'Neil**, seventeenth president (2019–22) presided for three years and guided the transition from founder-led nonprofit to new leadership.

- *10 Seconds*, the second piece in the **Theatre for Change** portfolio produced. **Luis Cardona** understood the value of the "*Oyeme* model" and urged consideration of a new play to help combat juvenile crime. Imagination Stage worked with County police chiefs **Thomas Manger** and **Marcus Jones** and later with the **DC Police Foundation** to create the new play. **Miriam Gonzalez** based the story on her observations between teens and police officers in drama exercises.
- *The Ballad of MuLan*, a collaboration with **Alvin Chan** and the Honolulu Theater for Youth, welcomed a delegation from the **Embassy of the People's Republic of China** to Opening Night to honor 40 years of Chinese–U.S. relations, and the fortieth anniversary of Imagination Stage.
- **Piano Theatre** welcomed – a Russian Theatre Company focused on the creative and social rehabilitation of hearing-impaired children.
- Partnership with **The Whittle School and Studios** – a proposed international network of private schools. Imagination Stage worked with WSS schools in China and DC.
- Third play in **Theatre for Change** portfolio, *Voices Beyond Bars* project launched, in partnership with the County Department of Health and Human Services at the County Correctional Facility.

2020 – **COVID-19** struck. Imagination Stage switched to on-line programming and offered access to classes and student and professional productions.

- Federal, state and county funding (private and public) ensured the **survival of Imagination Stage** during the pandemic shut down.

2021 – **Jason Najjoum** appointed by the board as managing director; Bonnie Fogel transitions to retirement.

- *10 Seconds* tour began, following the video version during COVID-19.

2022 – **Kim Woodson Barnette**, eighteenth president (2022–25), led the organization through staff and board training in inclusion, diversity, equity and access.

Appendix C: Who's Who

A quick reference to some of those mentioned in *Entrepreneurial Arts and Cultural Leadership* who helped Bethesda Academy of Performing Arts and Imagination Stage succeed.

- **Lisa Agogliati:** Established Imagination Stage's Deaf Access Company Program in 1991 which was awarded nine years of federal grants. Lisa previously served as dance faculty and accountant for BAPA.
- **Kim Greenfield Alfonso:** Fifteenth Imagination Stage president. Second Imagination Stage DC president.
- **Sally D. Bailey:** MFA, MSW, RDT/BCT. 1989 Founded BAPA Arts Access Program. Professor, director of graduate studies in theatre and director of the Drama Therapy Program, at Kansas State University.
- **Kim Woodson Barnette:** Imagination Stage DC third president; Imagination Stage eighteenth president. Project manager for LMI's team at NASA supporting Inclusion, Diversity Equity and Accessibility initiatives within their Science Mission Directorate.
- **Cathy Bernard:** Imagination Stage board member and angel investor. Head of HCM Corporation, a property management and investment firm. Business consultant. Creator of the Bernard/Ebb Songwriting Competition.
- **Richard Bradbury:** Imagination Stage producing artistic director for the Studio Theater 1997–2006. Olivet Boys and Girls Club Center for the Arts.
- **Robert G, Brewer, Jr.:** Imagination Stage eighth president (2000–03). Attorney: Lerch, Early and Brewer.
- **Kathryn "Kate" Chase Bryer:** BAPA faculty 1990. In 1991, created Imagination Stage's Theatre for Young Audiences at White Flint shopping center. Director of Theatre Imagination Stage. Independent director.
- **Judi Canter:** Capital campaign director 1999–2004.
- **Jane Fairweather:** Fourteenth Imagination Stage president (2013–15), first Imagination Stage DC president (2014). Realtor, the Jane Fairweather Team.
- **J.J. Finkelstein:** Seventh Imagination Stage president, 1998–2000. BioTech executive.

- **Cynthia Friedman:** Long-time Imagination Stage graphic design consultant and provider.
- **Barbara "Bobbie" Gottschalk:** Third president, 1990–92, co-founder Seeds of Peace.
- **Nancy T. Greenspan:** Fifth president 1994–96. Author.
- **Wendy Hamilton:** Associate director of Institutional Development 2002–07. Planned parenthood major gifts officer.
- **Stephen P. Hayes:** Tenth Imagination Stage president 2005–07. Raised Imagination Stage profile by introducing many dignitaries including Presidents George H.W. Bush and Barbara Bush; Laura Bush; Eunice Shriver. The great great grandson of President Rutherford B. Hayes.
- **Gail Humphies:** Interim artistic director (1988), board member, consultant. Author, arts administrator, director, Fulbright senior scholar; dean emerita College of Fellows of the American Theatre; dean emerita Stephens College; professor emerita The American University.
- **Caleen Synette Jennings:** BAPA faculty member, founder Black Kids in Theater (1988); Faculty emerita The American University, playwright.
- **Patricia Kratzer:** BAPA and Imagination Stage CFO (1999–2011). Playwright, director, actress.
- **David Markey:** BAPA Faculty. Imagination Stage director of education (2001–13). Deputy director, Commission on the Arts and Humanities Commission, Government of the District of Columbia.
- **Lynn Mattingly:** (1987–2000): First volunteer, director of education, co-writer of the proposal for the Forever Home. CIA project director.
- **Frank Allen Philpot, PhD:** First president of Bethesda Academy of Performing Arts, 1986–88. Former director of children's and family programming, PBS. Associate professor of marketing, George Mason University, VA.
- **Patrick O'Neil:** Imagination Stage seventeenth president. Attorney: Lerch, Early and Brewer.
- **Tim Reagan,** BAPA faculty, director of education (1989), later taught applied theatre and playback theatre. Expressive therapy drama therapist, Shady Grove Adventist Health Care Behavioral Health in Maryland.
- **Lucy Rockefeller Waletzky and Laurance S. Rockefeller:** Angel investors in BAPA and Imagination Stage for three decades.
- **Sally Rosenberg:** Ninth board president 2003–05. Ladybug productions. Playwright.
- **Christina Rutter** (2003–07): Volunteer coordinator. Apprentice. Marketing associate. Board. Board volunteer manager, San Francisco Symphony.
- **Donna Salamoff:** Associate director, Deaf Access Company, 1994–2004. Director of theatre at Sante Fe School for the Deaf.

- **Joanne Seelig Lamparter:** Student BAPA's Deaf Access company. 2014: director of education. 2023–present: Imagination Stage chief artistic programming officer.
- **Eugene "Gene" M. Smith:** Imagination Stage board member and Forever Home developer.
- **Marcia R. Smith:** Co-founder of Bethesda Academy of Performing Arts, executive director, Screen Actors Guild Foundation
- **Janet Stanford:** BAPA faculty. BAPA director of theatre. Imagination Stage founding artistic director 1993–2024. Author and playwright.
- **Jose Antonio Tijerino:** Imagination Stage board member led the Oyeme project. President and CEO, Hispanic Heritage Foundation.
- **Carol and Jim Trawick:** BAPA and Imagination Stage angel investors for decades. Paid down the construction loan on the Forever Home in 2008. Carol Trawick is an entrepreneur and social activist.

Appendix D: Board Responsibilities

Imagination Stage's Maryland and DC board members are responsible for major **policy, planning, budgeting, and advocacy** for the organization.

The boards as a whole:

- **Approve** the annual budget and audit and monitor progress against financial targets.
- **Act** on policies recommended by committees of the board or staff.
- **Advise** staff and committees on programming priorities.
- **Approve and monitor** strategic planning and roll-out.
- **Enhance** organizational brand: reputation and visibility and help broaden support.
- **Identify** and nurture relationships with new community members for positions on the board and/or committees or *Ad Hoc* task forces.
- **Advocate** on behalf of the organization.

Individual board members should:

- **Maintain** a passionate commitment to the mission and goals of the organization.
- **Attend** board meetings.
- **Serve** on at least one committee or task force, or have another special assignment.
- **Review** materials sent in advance of meetings and contribute to board discussions on critical policy issues.
- **Be knowledgeable** about the organization and be an effective ambassador and active promoter of Imagination Stage and Imagination Stage DC.
- **Be available** as an *ad hoc* advisor to the producing artistic director and senior staff when board members' personal skills and perspectives are needed.
- **Introduce** the organization to friends and colleagues, including new donors, patrons and potential board members.

- **Host** an opening of a professional show. This does not include financing the event, but represents an opportunity for the board member to invite a small group of guests for the performance and includes the option to host a pre-performance reception for those guests.
- **Attend** the Annual Gala and bring guests
- **Attend** a student performance.
- **Make a personal contribution of financial, social, cultural or other resource important to the enterprise.**

Appendix E: Board Management and Governance Toolkit

In Trait 3: "Igniting and Engaging" we discussed at length the necessity of a board and how building those relationships is crucial to an institution's success. But sometimes those tips are more easily said than done. Below, we've put together a toolkit to help you navigate the process.

First Steps: The New Board Member Orientation

Once your new board member slate has been voted in, send a letter to the new board members congratulating them, welcoming them and advising them of the date of their first board meeting.

When it comes time for the board member orientation, ask them to arrive two hours ahead of the full board meeting so that they can have their orientation. At Imagination Stage, we tried different scenarios for board orientations over the years, and you should too to determine what works best for your group. A social dinner followed by a business meeting is my preferred orientation process. However, we learned that our new board members preferred to have the orientation at the nonprofit on the same evening as their first board meeting.

Ahead of the first board meeting, new board members should have received several notifications advising them of all the board meetings that need to populate their calendars. At the first board meeting of the year, they are welcomed with whatever pomp and ceremony you can muster. I have seen board members publicly "sworn in" by an elected leader, which certainly added to the solemnity of the occasion. Your "welcome" also sends a message to continuing board members that board membership is an important responsibility. At Imagination Stage, we also publicly thank board members whose terms are ending with gifts and anecdotes. It's important to say thank you, and in extolling the virtues of those leaving, it gives another opportunity to underscore what makes a good board member.

There must be a formal agenda for the orientation. However, the priority goal is for the new board members to meet the board and staff leadership so that they feel welcomed. The small group setting allows them to get a sense of the leadership team with whom they will be working. To this end, all board members should also have name tags.

The board president, the governance chair and staff leadership must work together to ensure that the new board member's first experience – the board meeting – is engaging.

New board members must prioritize the orientation meeting on their calendars, and the prioritization of such meetings should be conveyed to them early on. If, for instance, they are traveling, they must attend virtually. The following 1.5-hour orientation agenda is suggested:

- President: welcome and introductions. Each person at the table says briefly why they are involved with Imagination Stage;
- Governance chair: goals for the orientation;
- Managing director: Imagination Stage 101;
- Artistic director: vision and programming for the upcoming year;
- Treasurer: financials;
- President of other member of the executive board: board roles and responsibilities;
- Development committee chair: fundraising opportunities;
- Governance committee: committee options to join.

All new board members will also be presented with the Board Handbook – I prefer a physical copy but a link to a board portal[30] should also be provided – to assure that they have what they need to understand their mandate, contents often include:

- Mission and organization overview,
- Board of Trustees' roles and responsibilities,
- Administrative policies and procedures,
- Board schedule,
- Committee descriptions,
- Bylaws organization,
- Budget organization,
- Staff organization chart and directory,
- Samples of program materials,
- Samples of management tools that help keep board members engaged. At Imagination Stage, these include:

- Board directory – a stapled document with photos and thumbnail sketches of all board members and leadership staff.
- Management dashboard – a one-sheet that shows the program and management goals for the upcoming year.
- Board briefs – a one sheet that staff leadership sends out on a weekly basis to all board members which keeps them informed of highs and lows in each organization area, and includes a list of things board members can help with.

Finally, it's a good idea to pair a new board member with a "board buddy," ideally someone from the governance committee. The board buddy introduces themselves to their pal at the board meeting, checks in with them afterward to see if they have any questions, and for the first year, checks in periodically after meetings or occasions. They also serve as a resource for the new board member.

Board Management: Cultivating and Maintaining the "Happily, Ever After"

Board management is a shared responsibility and should be divided among three people: board president, chair of the governance committee and staff executive.

Ultimately, what we've found is that board management comes down to board engagement. An engaged board is a healthy, active, fully functioning board. The basic strategy for success in board engagement is a clear and shared understanding of the board's oversight responsibility, the board member's personal goals and the nonprofit goals. These should be constantly reinforced orally and in materials.

At Imagination Stage, board and staff goals are tied to the three-year strategic plan. This plan, which is updated every two years, should be the result of comprehensive discussions between leadership staff and selected board members. Annually, staff leadership reviews the strategic plan and creates a one-sheet "Dashboard" for the year which identifies goals/outcomes for the upcoming year, assigns numerical goals and the staff point person for each goal. At Imagination Stage, an ongoing strategic plan goal is the engagement and nurturing of the Board of Trustees. This ensures that all who read the document are aware of the importance of the board in meeting organizational goals.

The engagement and motivation of board members will vary considerably depending upon the size and the maturity of the nonprofit. In the early days of the organization, board members will be very motivated and engaged because they know they are ensuring that the nonprofit will survive. Board members will be family members, clients and community supporters and they will be fully engaged in the cake sales, car washes and other events designed to fund the fledgling organization.

As the nonprofit stabilizes, more advanced skills will be required. No matter the nonprofit's place on the growth/maturation journey, the same basic strategies apply. They all involve providing opportunities for board members to achieve meaningful work for an organization whose mission they believe in alongside a group of like-minded people. Critically, they must feel that they and their work are truly valued by board and staff leadership alike.

The priority now is for board and staff leadership to foster authentic relationships between and among board and staff members. Board members will be more productive, engaged and motivated if they not only believe in the cause of the nonprofit but also if they LIKE the people with whom they serve. Hopefully, the work to maintain board member enthusiasm does not overtax staff.

We know that this doesn't happen and some effort goes into maintaining the board member's engagement. This can be a frustration for staff, with a constant sense of needing to bring the board member back into the fold. It doesn't need to be so. A few tools and strategies allow board monitoring, evaluation and engagement to take place in an organized fashion.

Enter the governance committee (GC). Many nonprofits don't even have this committee. Many simply have a nominating committee. As noted earlier, for board governance to be effective, there must be the kind of comprehensive oversight that can only be achieved by a fully functioning, effective governance committee. I consider this the most essential of all board committees since it oversees the people, and as we know, it's the people that make the organization hum like a well-honed engine. The nominating aspect of governance should be subsumed into the governance committee.

Your governance committee's primary task is ensuring the meaningful engagement of each and every board member.

The Governance Committee should maintain the following functions:

- Set schedules and agendas. Working with the board president and executive staff leadership, the governance committee assures that meetings will be productive, efficient and engaging. Agenda items should be led by board members when possible. Board members are more engaged when peers lead discussions. Ensure that there is sufficient time for networking before and after meetings.
- Ensure bylaws and other legal documents are updated regularly.
- Ensure year-round prospecting for new board members. Conduct interviews with prospects. Engage prospects on appropriate committees or task forces. Nominate prospects to the board. Conduct orientation of new board members.

- Ensure board members are engaged through such strategies as the "board pal/buddy system" where board members are mentored for the first year of their board service.
- Ensure regular (annual) board evaluation surveys to discover if board members feel that they, individually, are being productive and whether the board, as an entity, is meeting its fiduciary responsibilities.
- Evaluation.

Consider the efficacy of the full board and its committees and task forces on an annual basis. We advise an annual written survey of all board members. This can be a simple survey but should seek to ascertain how the board member feels about their engagement and whether the board as a whole is involved in those aspects of management that fall within its mandate. Imagination Stage sometimes hired an outside consultant to facilitate this. One year we were surprised to realize we had not been fully involving the board in our planning process. A clear oversight which we put right immediately.

Consider if all committees and task forces are serving as visualized, or if they should be streamlined, restructured, etc. More importantly, is the organization involved in new business areas that would benefit from additional oversight? For instance, when Imagination Stage became involved in providing access to children with physical and intellectual differences, we started an access committee. Most recently, new task forces have been formed to focus on issues relating to new endeavors in social justice work and in IDEA practice. This strategy ensures that the nonprofit's business continues to be adequately addressed.

Ongoing evaluation of each board member should also be part of the governance committees' remit. The easiest way to check on each board member's engagement is to maintain a simple board engagement grid (see Appendix F) which notes the following tangible aspects of each board member's contributions of time, treasure and talent. And is monitored at every GC meeting. The grid includes the following:

- Committee participation,
- Board meeting attendance,
- Special events support,
    - Fundraising – has the board member met their give-get? Does the board member bring other donor prospects and funds to the table?
    - Prospecting – has the board member introduced new board prospects?
- Other contributions.

Other strategies to ensure that board members stay engaged include:

- Build a board that board members want to be a part of to ensure engagement and attendance at meetings.

- In-person board and committee meetings: build in plenty of time for networking and socializing.
- Printed and electronic board/staff directory with headshots, bios, family information for all board and staff members to build community.
- Communications: board members have limited time and attention spans. The extent of the work of many nonprofits requires board member diligence to keep up to date. Board communications can help. These should be primarily electronic, strategic and coordinated (coming from one place). Communication practices can include the following emails:
  - o Monthly: calendar invites for events board members are requested to attend.
    - Population of board calendars. Send calendar invites that can easily be accepted, rather than relying on board members to pop into their own calendars. Busy board members can easily overlook this task.
    - Board briefs: weekly one-sheet overviews with one bullet point on each aspect of the organization. This one-sheet includes board action items ... things staff need help with. Also shout-outs onboard news: anniversaries, new jobs, etc. This is an Imagination Stage "Best Practice" which has been adopted by many and was one of the practices that won us recognition for nonprofit management.

Meeting venues: experiment with different locations for meetings. While it is important for board members to be accustomed to visiting the nonprofit's home, having meetings at other locations, including the homes of board members, will encourage attendance.

The board meeting: create an engaging agenda: there is nothing worse than being talked AT for hours.

- **Agenda** – send out ahead of the meeting, along with financials, consent agendas and anything else that is going to be discussed and where the opportunity for prior consideration will help board members be productive. (See a sample in Appendix H)
- Provide **networking** opportunities before and after with drinks and food. Get the food catered *pro bono* by a friendly neighborhood restaurant.
- Keep board meetings meaningful and relevant.
- **Consent agendas** (typically summaries of committee meetings) are emailed one week ahead of meetings, if there are no comments, they will be "read into the meeting notes" and this will save a lot of time. Questions on the consent agendas should be emailed to the chair of the committee and settled ahead of the meeting. Committee chairs ONLY bring committee items to the

full board if a discussion and a vote is required; otherwise, it all goes into the consent agenda.

- The governance chair presents the **consent agendas** at the top of the agenda, along with the minutes of the last meeting, asks if there are any questions and if there are none, the governance chair asks for a vote of approval for them to be included in the minutes.
- **Financials:** a full report on the financials should always be part of the board agenda. The financials should be sent ahead of the meeting and members with questions encouraged to connect with the board treasurer or staff leadership prior to the meeting.
- **Show your work:** always try to showcase the work of your organization, in a "brief but spectacular" manner.
- **Ensure participation:** include a topic for discussion, coach board and staff leadership in practices that invite participation. Staff and board reports are essential, but members don't want to be talked AT for the entire time. Ensure board members engage! This can be accomplished through 1–1 meetings with the board chair or leadership if people are not meeting their engagement agreements.
- **Structure a simple opportunity** for all board members to contribute. At Imagination Stage, we go around the table and ask members to say "What I Did for Imagination Stage" since the last meeting. This provides for "thanks" and also underscores that everyone should be doing something! Staff can also jump in if board members are reticent with their own recollections of what board members have contributed.
- **Announce and thank** board members who have been especially effective, celebrated a milestone. Use one board meeting a year to announce and reward staff milestones publicly (5–10–15–20 years).

Highly Structured Board Committees Lead to Engagement

Committees and task forces: this is where board members make friends and learn about the organization. Committee engagement is especially important on a large board where a board member might feel that what they can contribute is not so vital. One issue with a larger board is that it's a way of making a board member feel invisible. And it is easier to walk away from responsibilities if you think you are invisible.

Meetings: don't have meetings just because! Only have a meeting if there is something that must be achieved by the people on that specific committee. The only exception is the finance committee which must meet monthly to consider the financial health of the organization.

Structure meetings so that members receive a comprehensive insight into that aspect of the organization's work the committee is tasked with addressing. Additionally, every committee or task force should start with an organizational overview – a one-page synopsis of financing and programming highlights and lowlights delivered by the most senior staff associate on the committee. Through this strategy, board members get a regular overview of the organization's status. Committee goals are informed by the annual dashboard which is based on the strategic plan.

Special events: all board members must attend priority special events such as opening nights, galas or other significant events. This is the premier opportunity for board members to attend a wonderful event with their board member friends and an opportunity to introduce family members. And it's a chance to have some FUN! One of the many reasons board members join boards.

Ways to make board members part of the action: ask board members to help the development team by making calls to people who have made donations, to say "thank you." This is a wonderful way for board members to connect with the nonprofit's supporters. If board members are willing, they can make follow-up calls later in the cycle and ask for renewal gifts.

Term limits: many boards include people who have been with the organization for years, sometimes decades. It is understandable that a nonprofit does not want to lose a board asset. That said, best practices strongly suggest term limits for ALL board members. A three-year term is advised, with a second three-year term possible. After that, a board member MUST step off for at least a year. IF, the board member wishes to remain very involved, they can join a committee or task force as a "lay" member and be invited back on to the board after a year has passed – if a comprehensive conversation has taken place which results in an understanding that a new board term would be mutually beneficial. Imagination Stage grants permanent board benefits to former board presidents.

Continuing recognition: former Imagination Stage board presidents are invited to all board meetings and honored at the Gala's and other special events. When major announcements have been made from the gala stage, they are invited onto the stage and represent the continuing leadership of the organization. This shows our admiration for our past leaders and also sends a subtle message to the current board, staff and assembled dignitaries of the importance people have in the Imagination Stage success story.

Leadership Roles

As we stated in Trait 3, board members are the lifeblood of the organization, second only to staff. A well-functioning board helps determine the well-being of the organization and the furtherance of the mission. The board and staff, working in sync, determine the effectiveness of the nonprofit. Board motivation and engagement are a high priority for board governance and staff.

Board President

The president must be, first and last, a cheerleader! Their most important function is ensuring that all board members are enthusiastically engaged, that they feel valued and that their expertise is being used. Board members must never feel that their time is wasted. If time permits, the president might underscore their commitment to their board by attending the occasional committee or task force meetings. The president's energy and commitment to the mission must be strongly communicated at each board meeting. In the event that a board member seems disaffected, the board president may need to have an individual meeting. The board president must assure efficient and effective board meetings which will help ensure board member motivation and engagement. Boring board meetings are the kiss of death!

At the beginning of the board president's tenure, the board president creates a list of goals for their administration – what do they want/need to accomplish? This list should be at the back of the president's mind at every meeting – if not on the table! One Imagination Stage president had his list on an index card that he brought to every meeting! Similarly, the staff leader has an annual plan based on the three-year goals noted in the organization's strategic plans. The relationship between the president and the lead staff member determines the effectiveness of the board. Ideally, they meet in person, weekly.

At Imagination Stage, 24 hours prior to the weekly meeting, the staff leader emails a one-page template, composed of bullet points representing each aspect of the organization's annual plan, with each area updated to represent current status, upcoming challenges and opportunities. The one-sheet is headed by an A1 section that includes those issues that must be prioritized for the weekly discussion and don't necessarily fall within the confines of the annual plan.

These weekly meetings will be mutually beneficial. Board leadership will be fully aware of status, challenges and opportunities; staff leadership will feel supported. It's a great tactical strategy to ensure board fiduciary oversight. And a bond will be formed between the president and staff leadership that is critical to the success of the organization.

Further, the board president leads the executive committee meetings and sets the agenda. The board president is seen as the chief "cheer leader" for the board and should be involved in this aspect of leadership regularly.

Very importantly, the board president is responsible for the annual evaluation of the staff leader. This includes considering salary increases or bonuses. Ideally, the nonprofit has an annual evaluation process whereby the staff leader starts the process by completing a self-evaluation which is then forwarded to the board president for their completion. Following completion of the paperwork, the two should meet for a discussion of the year just passed and expectations for the year ahead. This process should occur well in advance of budget finalization so that salary increases can be included.

The power of the president cannot be overstated. The entrepreneurial leader recognizes this and ensures that they are in a tight partnership with the president every step of the way. This is not the same as an organization that relies on the president as an unpaid staff member to help with every last thing from bake sale to budget. Correctly deployed the president is the strongest strategic asset in the nonprofit's toolbox. That is the way it has always been at BAPA and at Imagination Stage.

Chair of the Governance Committee

The chair of the governance committee is second only to the board president in ensuring the engagement of the board and board members as individual participants. The chair of this committee must alert the board president, executive committee and ultimately the full board if they find (through the committee's evaluation procedures) that changes to the board structure or practice need to be addressed. A similar relationship should be built between the governance chair and the staff leader responsible for governance.

To ensure optimum functioning, staff leadership should meet with the governance chair at the beginning of the year to ensure that the committee's work for the year will be informed by not only its traditional responsibilities but also the annual priorities as laid out in the strategic plan.

Working together, staff leadership and the governance chair will schedule the committee meetings for the year to assure that their work syncs with board timelines and to ensure that each item on the committee's mandate will be covered annually. Staff leadership and the governance chair should also meet ahead of committee meetings to refine the agenda.

Director of Development

The chief development officer must dedicate a significant percentage of their time to board prospecting, engaging and motivation. Talking to board members ONLY when it is time for them to underwrite the gala, or pay annual dues, is never a good idea. Ideally, one-on-one conversations happen regularly with every board member. The director of development similarly encourages their development team to be similarly gracious and personable with board members. Besides cultivating the human touch, the director of development creates tools (besides the governance committee grid) that measure the engagement of board members, ensure regular electronic communications, consider which new projects interest which board members and follow up. The excellent director of development considers their board members part of their development team and includes them in their thinking.

Fundraising Committee

If you can form and maintain an effective fund-raising committee, one which includes board members who focus on events, others who focus on business or individual contacts this is a great tool for board engagement. Imagination Stage has used several models and found that its board members prefer to be on committees that build relationships (business and community engagement committees) or on special events committees (Gala's, Festivals, etc.). This is an example of how one must always evaluate committee effectiveness. Ultimately, no committee will be effective if you don't have a strong committee chair.

Committee Chairs' Roles

Effective committee chairs create agendas that:

- ensure staff gets the support needed in the areas of their committee oversight,
- provide opportunities for board members to network with each other and bond with staff associates,
- ensure that executive leadership provides a five-minute organizational update at the top of every meeting to ensure that board members have a full understanding of the organization's status and to provide context for decisions to be made in the meeting that will follow.

Following the meeting, executive leadership and the chair meet to consider follow-up actions.

Committee chairs should be mindful of the importance of ensuring that these relationships are maximized. Some committee chairs will have one meeting at their own homes. These kinds of meetings are among the most meaningful events and help assure strong friendships are built among board members.

Staff Associate Roles

If board members are also clients of the nonprofit, their deepest relationships may be with staff associates. It therefore behooves staff associates to ensure that board members' understanding of the organization's work is maximized. These board members may be the most knowledgeable about the organization's work, and, therefore, among the most resourceful of board members. Additionally, staff associates often are the ones taking the minutes during a meeting while the secretary engages in the discussions.

Staff Leadership Role

The staff associate who leads the organization must set aside at least 10% of their time each week to maintain board members' engagement and motivation. An annual, private, check-in with each board member – perhaps over coffee, lunch, drinks is recommended. In a free-ranging conversation, and one that focuses on the board member, new discoveries about the board member's interests, abilities, associates will invariably lead to a more valuable relationship. I have found time and time again that in these kinds of meetings, I discovered things about a board member that proved to be a remarkable asset to the organization.

First and last: board and staff must value board members – and show it in word and deed.

Appendix F:
Board Member Engagement Grid

The image below is a picture of the engagement grid. It would be maintained in a spreadsheet with the board members' names in the first column (not shown for privacy).

Term			Committees & Task Forces										ON Host	FY21 Gala Attend	Student Perf.	Give/Get Met	Kick-off	Board2	Board3	AGM
FY21	FY22	FY23	Finance	Governance	CE	Executive	Strategic	ISDC	TF C	Oyeme	Gala	C B								
T2	T2	T2				M										Yes	X			
T2	T2					M	M	Liasion			Chair					Yes		X	X	
T2						M	M									No	X	X	X	
T2	T2			M												Yes	X		X	
T1	T2	T2				M										No	X		X	
T1	T1	T1	M						M							No	X	X	X	
T1	T1	T1			M											No		X	X	
T2	T2	T2				M	M				Chair					Yes	X	X	X	
T2			M													No	X		X	
T1	T1	T2		M												Yes	X	X	X	
T1	T1	T1			M											No	X	X	X	
T1	T1	T2	M	M												Yes	X	X	X	
																	X	X		
T1	T1	T2							M							Yes	X	X	X	
T1	T1	T1	M													No	X			
T1	T1	T2	M													No	X	X		
T2	T2	T2	M				M									No	X	X	X	
T1	T1	T2			Chair											No	X			
T1	T1	T1			M											No	X	X	X	
T1	T1	T2			M											No	X	X	X	
T1	T2	T2														No	X		X	
T1	T2	T2														No	X	X	X	
T2	T2	T2		M												No				
T1	T2	T2	Chair			M										No	X	X		

Appendix G: Annual Strategic Goal Dashboard Sample

The dashboard is headed by the assumptions that will be broken down in the grid. ASSUMPTIONS for FY ____, the five strategic areas that will be monitored and evaluated during the year.

The grid looks something like this:

Goals*	**Measurable objectives**	**Actions to achieve goals**	**Staff/board responsible**	**Monthly update on goal meeting**
Strategic planning	One three-year strategic plan to be evaluated every year	Convene meeting of appropriate board and staff	Managing director Board strat plan leader	
Economic sustainability	Balanced budget, six-month reserves, comprehensive financial reporting showing three-month trends, cash flow, unit economics	Monthly meetings of board committee weekly staff meetings	Staff executive Board treasurer Board president	
Program area 1	Achieve these metrics:	Organization specific	Staff in charge of the program area	
Program area 2	Achieve these metrics:	Organization specific	Staff in charge of the program area	
IDEA	Achieve these metrics:	Organization specific	Staff in charge of the program area	

Goals*	**Measurable objectives**	**Actions to achieve goals**	**Staff/board responsible**	**Monthly update on goal meeting**
Staff support	Ensure 100% staff satisfaction that their needs are addressed via regular meetings, reviews, check-ins		Staff leadership	
Board support	Ensure 100% board member engagement as indicated by recommended financial support, committee and board attendance, etc.		Staff leadership Development director Board president Board committee chairs	

*Examples are taken from the organization's strategic plan to achieve its goals.

Appendix H: Sample Board Meeting Agenda

A board agenda might look something like this. Board and staff leadership should ensure there is an opportunity to engage all board members by providing: network opportunities, a chance to further engage with the work, a chance to discuss issues and a chance for everyone to speak. Please note the reporting is split between board and staff leadership. Agenda, consent agendas, finances, and *Who Knows Who* (a list of people we want to meet) have been sent 48 hours ahead.

	Meeting of the Board of Trustees Imagination Stage March 20, 20__ 6:00–8:00 p.m. in Studio A 6:00–6:30 Networking Reception Courtesy of Sponsor Café	
6:30	Welcome and Opening Remarks	John Big, board president
6:35	Minutes and Consent Agendas	Jane Apex, governance chair
6:40	Programs and Productions: Status	Mandy Play, artistic director
6:50	**Finances**	
	• Overview	Susie Dollar, treasurer
	• Monthly report	James Bucks, managing director
	• Audit report	S. Dollar
	• Budget 20__ : VOTE REQUIRED	S. Dollar
7:05	**Fundraising Update**	
	• Annual Goals	Nelly Grant, development staff
	• Gala: May 10	M. Priestly and M. Quant, chairs
7:10	**Who Knows Who (board prospects)**	J Apex, governance chair
7:15	Program update	
	• New program DISCUSSION	Mary Practice, education director

7:20	Sharing our work/mission/values*	M. Play, artistic director
7:45	What have I done for IStage lately?**	All board members
7:55	Closure and calendar	John Big

Drinks and Dessert in the Lobby

* Report includes an opportunity for a five-minute sharing of student work.

** An opportunity for all board members to share how they have helped the organization.

Appendix I: Sample Weekly Board Report (aka Bonnie's Board Briefs)

[Ed: FY21 items are tied to Strategic Plan and Management Dashboard]

A1 (Items not on the strategic plan):
Financials:

- CFO projection of $ – deficit needs some additional phrasing, or contextualizing BEFORE presentation to the board. The audit will not reflect this due to the PPP crisis funding. We anticipate going into the line of credit in July (as is customary).

Gala update:

- We will hit the original financial goal – which is very good news.
- Artistic leadership doing a great job on the programming.

Warehouse:

- Contract is up on rental in July.
- Opportunity for a new three-year contract at a discount.
- Opportunity to buy something now with savings.

Personnel:

- Three strategically timed (!) babies on the way. (1) JP out Jan–April. Laurie Levy Page hired as interim. (2) CC out March–June. Will need to hire lower-level support. (3) JS out June–Sept. Do not anticipate over-hire.

STRATEGIC GOALS FOR FY 21

(1) STRATEGIC PLAN: CREATE A NEW THREE-YEAR PLAN

- Board committee chair thinks we should wait.
- BF thinks we should begin first ¼ FY21.
- Build on fall staff retreat which went very well. Everyone felt empowered.

- Messaging increasingly important. Board member MJ has done an excellent job. She will oversee web implementation and will roll out the messaging.
- Board member MW has agreed to help with Strat Plan first ¼ FY21.

(2) LEADERSHIP TRANSITION

- On track

(3) ECONOMIC SUSTAINABILITY/RISK MANAGEMENT

- FY21: sufficient cash right now. If we continue into the second quarter w/o the possibility of in-person classes or shows, we will have a problem.
- Right now, the government is stepping up and keeping us afloat.
- New funding from government Tourism grants anticipated.

(4) LERNER THEATRE: STAGE HIGH-QUALITY THEATRE THAT IS ACCESSIBLE DURING THE PANDEMIC

- *Snow Queen* digital offerings include prequel for families and workshops for schools. Excellent and exciting work but not a lot of sales.
- *Spy Academy:* digital gaming show – rolling out in February.
- Theatre for very young audiences – hoping for in-person this summer.

(5) EDUCATION: FOSTER AND SUSTAIN RELATIONSHIPS AND BUILD NEW ONES DURING THE PANDEMIC

- Fall **EDUCATION:** So far, registrations are acceptable [...] about 55% of the goal. We hope to bring in more interest for the second session, but we do not expect to meet the fall goal.
- **DC Education:** JS expects to hit the goal thanks to several contracts for virtual from DC schools.

(6) THEATRE FOR CHANGE: EXPLORE COMPLEX SOCIAL ISSUES

- **TEN SECONDS:**
    - Meetings with council members went well. Follow-up sent.
    - Council member GA going to help strategize on the next steps, especially police department funding for alternative law enforcement activities.
    - *Ten seconds* will be:
        - Virtual premiere of the video in DC and hopefully MoCo: March/April.
        - In Fall: In-person premiere with celebrities BW and/ or TS. Do it at MLK in DC and possibly Up-County in MoCo.
        - We will host an online program once the film is out with a panel, etc. that anyone can join.

    - AR engaged on the Theatre for Change committee, she is very eager to help with ten seconds.
- **OYEME II** – in the works, funding achieved.
- **VOICES BEYOND BARS** – going forward digitally, very successful. Funding achieved.

(7) **IMAGINATION STAGE DC**

- Board leadership excellent, the board is enthusiastic.
- There are opportunities this year for ten seconds, for more education sites, we hope to bring DC kids to IStage instead of going to DC theatres – as an interim measure.

(8) **EQUITY DIVERSITY INCLUSION: Move Imagination Stage Forward on the EDI Continuum**

- We have a working task force: lots of appropriate reading happening: leadership learning and book club; this is a major goal on our management dashboard for FY21.
- We have a very enthusiastic team whose aspirations we are trying to temper. We will bring any policy changes to the exec committee – such as land acknowledgments.
- We need to prioritize the board in these discussions.
- Going to TYA EDI meetings is a good start.

Appendix J:
Arts Access Program Logic Model

Target Population: Middle school students from KEEN and Imagination Stage

Program goal: 15 students + 15 facilitators in a puppet/theatre camp with show

Inputs (Resources for program)	Activities (Services)	Outputs (# of activities, participants)	Outcomes (How will the client change because of this program?)		
			Initial	Intermediate	Longer-Term
Imagination Stage • Staff time • Project management • Musicians • Theatre teaching staff • Inclusion training • Project video documentation • Research data collection & analysis (work with specialists) • Puppet Co. • Admin • Lead artists • Supplies **KEEN** • Staff time • Students/recruitment • Teen mentors (Aner Phase I) **Cleo-Echo Park** • Staff time • Classroom space • Food/supplies coordination • Space logisitcs	**Phase I (Planning & Recruitment)** • Plan specific actions/dates for recruitment & training • Recruit team of H.S. students • Video record recruitment process • Hire lead artists • Hire teaching staff & musicians • Finalize research component **Phase II (Training)** • Inclusion training for teen mentors • Inclusion training for artists and teachers • Curriculum development: teens & lead artists, teachers • Recruitment of M.S. youth participants • 4 visits to Puppet Co to see shows by potential recruits • Video record !raining and visits **Phase III (Spring Program Delivery)** • Parent Orientation • 6 weeks of after school skills building for MS • Team building workshops & Trips • Artists and teachers: determine artistic frameworks and puppet media for final project • Video record workshops and trips **Phase IV (Summer Camp)** • Regular focus area group meetings • Visual - Design set, props, costumes • Performing- acting workshops, movement workshops, finalize script. • Puppet Completion and rehearsal • Distribution of healthy snacks each day • Video record process aod product • Implementation of final production	• MS students gain confidence and skills through puppetry and performance • HS students gain inclusion/ facilitation skills within an arts setting • Regular participation by M.S students (15- 20) during phase III - V • Creation of a DVD/Video or the process and final product for parents, for data analysis, and for presentation at conferences or online • Creation of a final product (Theatre with Puppetry piece) that all constituents can feel proud or • Research/survey • indicators that study the hypothesis that the arts, including puppetry, provide a mode of expression for students with disabilities or with autism who otherwise struggle to communicate. • Teamwork and confidence building are secondary data sets	• The MS students will gain skills and a desire to create with puppets and theatre as a mode of expression. • The KEEN community will discover a new outlet for their clients through the arts, specifically puppetry and theatre • The MS and HS students working as facilitators or participants will gain a greater understanding of the process and importance of inclusion • Families of MS students will see the arts as an opt ion to provide greater confidence and creativity for their children		• Families of MS and HS students will see a greater degree of confidence • MS students will, without a puppet intermediary, demonstrate gains in communication with others • Report to stakeholders the data results to the hypothesis that the mts, including puppetry, offer a mode of expression for students with disabilities or with autisim who otherwise struggle to communicate. Teamwork and confidence building are secondary areas of potential analysis.

Endnotes

INTRODUCTION

1. Arts & Economic Prosperity 6, "Welcome | Arts & Economic Prosperity 6 (AEP6)."
2. Audience Outlook Monitor, accessed November 15, 2024, https://www.audienceoutlook-monitor.com/covid19-archive.
3. Wingo, "What Are the Different Types of Nonprofits?"
4. Byrnes, *Management and the Arts.*
5. Rosewall, *Arts Management: Uniting Arts and Audiences in the 21st Century.*
6. Kaiser, *Strategic Planning in the Arts.*
7. Stein et al., *Performing Arts Management (Second Edition): A Handbook of Professional Practices.*
8. Chmelik, *Museum Operations.*
9. Schulman, *Artpreneur.*
10. Beer, *Artrepreneur.*
11. Ries, *The Lean Startup.*
12. Kim, *Blue Ocean Strategy*, 17.

TRAIT 1. THE VISION THING: THE ENTREPRENEURIAL LEADERSHIP IMPERATIVE

13. Collins and Porras, "Building Your Company's Vision."
14. Board Source, "9 Characteristics of a Mission Statement."
15. Di Giulio and Giulio, "Are Leaders Born or Made?"
16. Collins, *Built to Last: Successful Habits of Visionary Companies.*
17. Weiner, *The Socrates Express.*
18. In 1979, the Bethesda Academy for Performing Arts (BAPA) was incorporated as a nonprofit organization. When it added a second location to begin a professional theatre for young audiences, the theatre was named BAPA's Imagination Stage. When BAPA moved to its Forever Home at 4908 Auburn Ave, Bethesda, Maryland, it adopted one name: Imagination Stage. This was official with paperwork filed at the state of Maryland and the Internal Revenue Service to recognize the name change legally.

TRAIT 2. IT'S ALL ABOUT THE PEOPLE: STAFF AND BOARD

19. Fisher and Phillips, *Work Better Together*, 209.
20. U.S. Bureau of Labor Statistics, "Economic News Release."
21. Robertson, *Holacracy*.

TRAIT 3. IGNITING AND ENGAGING: ENTREPRENEURIAL LEADERSHIP AND THE BOARD

22. *Non Profit News | Nonprofit Quarterly*, "A Guide for Nonprofits on Board Governance."

TRAIT 5. THE POWER OF YOUR VOICE AND ADVOCACY

23. Merriam-Webster, s.v. "advocacy," accessed November 21, 2024, https://www.merriam-webster.com/dictionary/advocacy.

TRAIT 6. THE ENTREPRENEURIAL BALANCE RISK VS. OPPORTUNITY

24. Johnson and Blanchard, *Who Moved My Cheese.*
25. Collins, *Built to Last: Successful Habits of Visionary Companies.*
26. The SWOT framework is credited to **Albert Humphrey**, who developed the approach at the Stanford Research Institute in the 1960s and early 1970s. It is still taught and used by businesses around the world. The core idea is that by evaluating your strengths, weaknesses, opportunities and threats you can chart your best strategies. Or as noted in the following proverb: "You cannot direct the wind, but you can adjust your sail."
27. Gardner, *Multiple Intelligences.*
28. Mardirosian and Lewis, *Arts Integration in Education.*

APPENDIX A: THE ORIGIN STORY

29. Laurence Rockefeller was an American businessman, financier, philanthropist and conservationist. He served as a trustee of the Rockefeller Brothers Fund, and as such provided venture capital for many successful start-ups.

APPENDIX E: BOARD MANAGEMENT AND GOVERNANCE TOOLKIT

30. Board Portals are emerging everywhere and can be easily created with folder and calendar permissions in a Google Workplace for a small organization. Some ideas for the why of Board Portals can be found here: https://static1.squarespace.com/static/51d98be2e4b05a25fc200cbc/t/539b2e43e4b0158bb074ecb6/1402678851803/ErinWagner_TechnologiesForBoardEngagement.pdf. Accessed November 15, 2024.

Bibliography and Additional Resources

INTRODUCTION

Admin. "What Do Arts Leaders Really Need?" *Hewlett Foundation* (blog), March 10, 2016. https://hewlett.org/what-do-arts-leaders-really-need/.

Americans for the Arts. "Arts & Economic Prosperity 6," October 25, 2021. https://www.americansforthearts.org/by-program/reports-and-data/research-studies-publications/arts-economic-prosperity-6.

Arts & Economic Prosperity 6. "Welcome | Arts & Economic Prosperity 6 (AEP6)." Accessed December 20, 2023. https://aep6.americansforthearts.org//.

Byrnes, William J. *Management and the Arts*. New York: Routledge, 2022.

Carter, Kate. "5 Reasons Why Leaders Are Made Not Born." *Text. HRZone*, January 16, 2019. https://www.hrzone.com/community/blogs/engage-in-learning/5-reasons-why-leaders-are-made-not-born.

Caust, Josephine. *Arts Leadership in Contemporary Contexts*. London: Routledge, 2020.

Chmelik, Samantha. *Museum Operations: A Handbook of Tools, Templates, and Models*. Lanham, Boulder, New York and London: Rowman & Littlefield Publishers, 2017.

Clark, Mark A., and Meredith Persily Lamel. *Six Paths of Leadership*. 1st ed. Cham: Palgrave Macmillan, 2021.

Cohen, William A. *Drucker on Leadership: New Lessons from the Father of Modern Management*. 1st ed. San Francisco, CA: Jossey-Bass, 2009.

DGCG Support. "2021 State of the Nonprofit Sector: The Painful, the Extraordinary and What's Next." Nonprofit Leadership Center of Tampa Bay, October 14, 2021. https://nlctb.org/news/2021-state-of-the-nonprofit-sector-the-painful-the-extraordinary-and-whats-next/.

Gardner, Howard E. *Multiple Intelligences: The Theory in Practice, a Reader*. New York: Basic Books, 1993.

Hogarth, Ruth. "Theatre's Model Is Broken." ArtsProfessional, August 24, 2023. https://www.artsprofessional.co.uk/magazine/news-comment/theatres-model-broken.

Kaiser, Michael M., and Brett E. Egan. *The Cycle: A Practical Approach to Managing Arts Organizations*. 1st ed. Waltham: Brandeis University Press, 2013.

Mondello, Bob. "Across the U.S., Regional Theaters Are Starting to Transform. Here's Why." *NPR*, September 21, 2022. https://www.npr.org/2022/09/21/1123177992/american-theater-is-changing-heres-why.

Rhine, Anthony. *Theatre Management: Arts Leadership for the 21st Century*. 1st ed. London: Red Globe Press, 2018.

Roedel, Jemma. *She Thinks Like a Boss Leadership*. N.p.: Jemma Roedel, 2021.

Schulman, Miriam. *Artpreneur: The Step-by-Step Guide to Making a Sustainable Living from Your Creativity*. New York: HarperCollins Leadership, 2023.

Stein, Tobie S., Jessica Rae Bathurst, Renee Lasher and Donna Walker-Kuhne Esq. *Performing Arts Management: A Handbook of Professional Practices*. 2nd ed. New York: Allworth, 2022.

Webb, Duncan. *Running Theatres*. 2nd ed. New York: Allworth, 2020.

Wingo, Lauren. "What Are the Different Types of Nonprofits?" U.S. Chamber of Commerce, February 5, 2021. https://www.uschamber.com/co/start/strategy/nonprofit-designations-explained.

TRAIT 1. THE VISION THING: THE ENTREPRENEURIAL LEADERSHIP IMPERATIVE

Andersson, Fredrik O. "A New Focus on Nonprofit Entrepreneurship Research." *Nonprofit Management and Leadership* 28, no. 2 (2017): 249–58. https://doi.org/10.1002/nml.21271.

Andersson, Fredrik O. "Nascent Nonprofit Entrepreneurship: Exploring the Formative Stage of Emerging Nonprofit Organizations." *Nonprofit and Voluntary Sector Quarterly* 45, no. 4 (August 2016): 806–24. https://doi.org/10.1177/0899764015603203.

Bailey, Sally. *Wings to Fly: Bringing Theatre Arts to Students with Special Needs*. Rockville: Woodbine House, 1993.

Bailey, Sally. *Drama in the Inclusive Classroom: Activities to Support Curriculum and Social Emotional Learning*. 1st ed. London: Routledge, 2021.

Bailey, Sally, ed. *Perform: Creative Arts Therapy Careers: Succeeding as a Creative Professional*. 1st ed. London: Routledge, 2021.

Bailey, Sally. *The Drama Decision Tree: Connecting Drama Therapy Interventions to Treatment*. 2nd ed. Bristol: Intellect, 2024.

Bailey, Sally, and Lisa Agogliati. "Dreams to Sign." Bedford, IN: US Department of Education & Imagination Stage, 2002.

Barrier-Free Theatre: Including Everyone in Theatre Arts – in Schools, Recreation, and Arts Programs – Regardless of (Dis)Ability. Bedford, IN: Idyll Arbor, 2010.

Beer, Lukas De. *Artrepreneur: A Field Guide for Creative Professionals*. N.p.: CreateSpace Independent Publishing Platform, 2016.

Business Insights Blog. "10 Characteristics of Successful Entrepreneurs | HBS Online," July 7, 2020. https://online.hbs.edu/blog/post/characteristics-of-successful-entrepreneurs.

Collins, Jim. *Built to Last: Successful Habits of Visionary Companies*. New York: Harper Collins, 1994.

Collins, Jim. *Good to Great*. New York: HarperCollins, 2001.

Collins, Jim, and Jerry I. Porras. "Building Your Company's Vision." *Harvard Business Review*, October 1996. https://hbr.org/1996/09/building-your-companys-vision.

Di Giulio, Justin. "Are Leaders Born or Made?," January 1, 2014. https://www.researchgate.net/publication/270684591_Are_leaders_born_or_made.

Duermyer, Randy. "What Is an Entrepreneur?" The Balance, May 22, 2024 (updated). https://www.thebalancemoney.com/entrepreneur-what-is-an-entrepreneur-1794303.

Dweck, Carol. *Mindset: The New Psychology of Success*. New York: Random House, 2006.

Johnson, Spencer, and Kenneth Blanchard. *Who Moved My Cheese*. 10th ed. New York: G. P. Putnam's Sons, 1998.

Kim, W. Chan, and Renee Mauborgne. *Blue Ocean Strategy: How to Create Uncontested Market Space and Make the Competition Irrelevant*. Boston: Harvard Business School Press, 2005.

Mardirosian, Gail Humphries, and Yvonne Pelletier Lewis. *Arts Integration in Education: Teachers and Teaching Artists As Agents of Change*. Bristol: Intellect, 2018.

Ries, Eric. *The Lean Startup: How Today's Entrepreneurs Use Continuous Innovation to Create Radically Successful Businesses*. New York: Crown, 2011.

Schueller, Jessica, and Hugo Figueiredo. "Adaptability Is Set to Be the Key Skill for the Future." *University World News*, July 3, 2021. https://www.universityworldnews.com/post.php?story=20210702110012289.

Stein, Tobie. *Leadership in the Performing Arts*. 1st ed. New York: Allworth, 2016.

Thurman, Rosetta. "Preparing the Next Generation of Nonprofit Leaders (SSIR)." *Stanford SOCIAL INNOVATION Review*, December 19, 2007. https://ssir.org/articles/entry/preparing_the_next_generation_of_nonprofit_leaders.

Weiner, Eric. *The Socrates Express: In Search of Life Lessons from Dead Philosophers*. New York: Simon and Schuster, 2021.

Woronkowicz, Joanna. "Arts, Entrepreneurship, and Innovation." *Journal of Cultural Economics* 45, no. 4 (December 2021): 519–26. https://doi.org/10.1007/s10824-021-09432-5.

Woronkowicz, Joanna, Douglas Noonan and Kelly LeRoux. "Entrepreneurship among Nonprofit Arts Organizations: Substituting between Wage and Flexible Labor." *Public Administration Review* 80, no. 3 (2020): 473–81. https://doi.org/10.1111/puar.13110.

TRAIT 2. IT'S ALL ABOUT THE PEOPLE: STAFF AND BOARD

Collins, Jim. *Built to Last: Successful Habits of Visionary Companies*. New York: William Collins, 1994.

Collins, Jim. *Good to Great*. New York: HarperCollins, 2001.

Economy, Peter. "19 Empowering Quotes From Oprah Winfrey." *Inc.*, May 20, 2015. https://www.inc.com/peter-economy/oprah-winfrey-19-inspiring-power-quotes-for-success.html.

Fisher, Jen, and Anh Nguyen Phillips. *Work Better Together: How to Cultivate Strong Relationships to Maximize Well-Being and Boost Bottom Lines*. New York: McGraw Hill Professional, 2021.

Hait, Andrew W. "The Majority of U.S. Businesses Have Fewer than Five Employees." United Staes Census Bureau, January 19, 2021. https://www.census.gov/library/stories/2021/01/what-is-a-small-business.html.

McKinsey & Company. "Our Insights – People & Organizational Performance." Accessed May 22, 2023. https://www.mckinsey.com/capabilities/people-and-organizational-performance/our-insights.

Morelli, Manuela. "The Next Generation of Leaders in No-Profit Sector." *Journal of Human Resource and Sustainability Studies* 4, no. 1 (January 2016): 50–53. https://www.scirp.org/journal/paperinformation?paperid=65247.

Press Office. "News Release 'Employee Tenure 2022.'" *Bureau of Labor Statistics*, September 22, 2022.

Robertson, Brian J. *Holacracy: The New Management System for a Rapidly Changing World.* London: Henry Holt and Company, 2015.

U.S. Bureau of Labor Statistics. "Economic News Release." September 26, 2024. https://www.bls.gov/news.release/tenure.nr0.htm.

TRAIT 3. IGNITING AND ENGAGING: ENTREPRENEURIAL LEADERSHIP AND THE BOARD

Bell, Jeanne, and *Nonprofit Quarterly*. "Beyond the Board Statement: How Can Boards Join the Movement for Racial Justice? (Part Two)." *Non Profit News | Nonprofit Quarterly*, July 1, 2020. https://nonprofitquarterly.org/beyond-the-board-statement-how-can-boards-join-the-movement-for-racial-justice-part-two/.

Board Source. "9 Characteristics of a Mission Statement." Accessed September 2013, https://boardsource.org/mission-statement-characteristics/.

BoardSource. "Homepage." Accessed December 10, 2023. https://boardsource.org/.

Carter, Ellis. "Top 10 Nonprofit Governance Mistakes." Charity Lawyer Blog, September 12, 2009. https://charitylawyerblog.com/2009/09/12/top-ten-non-profit-governance-mistakes/.

Ingraham, Patricia W. *The Art of Governance: Analyzing Management and Administration.* 1st ed. Washington: Laurence E. Georgetown University Press, 2004.

Masaoka, Jan. "Ditch Your Board Composition Matrix." *Blue Avocado*, June 12, 2012. https://blueavocado.org/board-of-directors/ditch-your-board-composition-matrix/.

Non Profit News | Nonprofit Quarterly. "What Is Governance? A Guide for Nonprofits on Board Governance," June 9, 2017. https://nonprofitquarterly.org/what-is-governance-definition/.

Price, Nick. "Nonprofit Laws Checklist for Board Members." BoardEffect (blog), October 25, 2022. https://www.boardeffect.com/blog/nonprofit-laws-checklist-for-board-members/.

Shekshnia, Stanislav. "How to Be a Good Board Chair." *Harvard Business Review*, March 1, 2018. https://hbr.org/2018/03/how-to-be-a-good-board-chair.

The Editors. "What Is Governance? A Guide for Nonprofits on Board Governance." *Non Profit News | Nonprofit Quarterly*, June 9, 2017. https://nonprofitquarterly.org/what-is-governance-definition/.

TRG Arts, and Jill Robinson. "Is Your GOVERNANCE on Auto-Pilot? | TRG 30." YouTube, September 24, 2020. https://www.youtube.com/watch?v=Q9Xy47XTnc4.

TRAIT 4. MAKING THE DIFFERENCE: PARTNERSHIPS AND COMMUNITY

Fisher, Jen, and Anh Nguyen Phillips. *Work Better Together: How to Cultivate Strong Relationships to Maximize Well-Being and Boost Bottom Lines*. New York: McGraw Hill Professional, 2021.

Kim, W. Chan, and Renee Mauborgne. *Blue Ocean Strategy: How to Create Uncontested Market Space and Make the Competition Irrelevant*. Boston: Harvard Business School Press, 2005.

TRAIT 5. THE POWER OF YOUR VOICE AND ADVOCACY

Brinckmeyer, Lynn. "Advocacy for the Arts: Forging Our Way Forward." *The Choral Journal*, 61, no. 1 (2020): 49–58.

TRAIT 6. THE ENTREPRENEURIAL BALANCE: RISK VS. OPPORTUNITY

Kim, W. Chan, and Renee Mauborgne. *Blue Ocean Strategy: How to Create Uncontested Market Space and Make the Competition Irrelevant*. Boston: Harvard Business School Press, 2005.

About the Authors

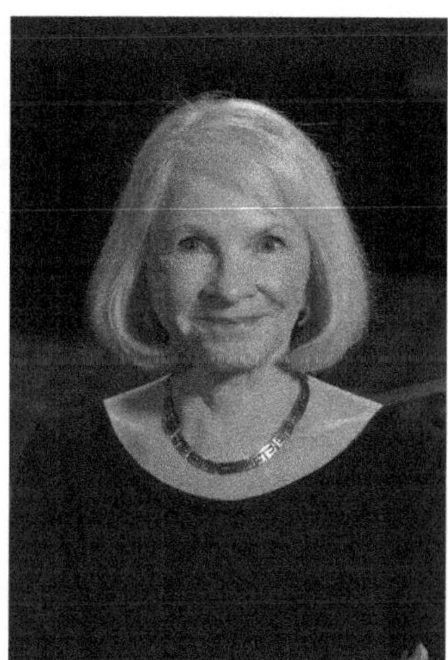

Bonnie Fogel. Courtesy of Imagination Stage.

Bonnie Fogel is a nonprofit leader responsible for creating, building and leading one of the top Theatres for Young Audiences in the United States for over four decades: Imagination Stage, Inc.

Her entrepreneurial approach touches upon many of the core business principles shared by nonprofits and for-profits alike. Over 43 years, Imagination Stage's influence as a Theatre for Young Audiences, an arts education exemplar, and a model for sustainable growth, has expanded across the country thanks to her founding entrepreneurial vision and intentional deployment of entrepreneurial leadership traits.

As the executive head of the organization, Bonnie was responsible for advancing the vision and mission of Imagination Stage by leading and overseeing all aspects of the organization. Her entrepreneurial style, developed in the marketing division of Marks & Spencer, the UK-based retail giant, informed her leadership style, which emphasized strategic direction, marketing and communications, and finding and supporting the resources (financial and human) needed to enhance the growth and development of a successful business. She worked closely with artistic and educational colleagues to ensure programming goals advanced the company's mission and vision while personally prioritizing efficient daily operation and administration, advocacy (political and entrepreneurial) strategic planning, fundraising, marketing, community relations, and governance by engaging boards of trustees, elected and appointed government officials, donors, and other community partners to support organization objectives. Bonnie was also instrumental in the establishment of Imagination Stage DC (in 2003). She is currently working as an arts management consultant and coach for nonprofit businesses.

When Imagination Stage was established (as Bethesda Academy of Performing Arts), Bonnie didn't have any of the skills that traditional wisdom dictates are necessary for success (for instance, she had not attended college or university) but she did have things that ended up being much more important:

- *A dream*: she knew what was missing in the community – opportunities for children to experience theatre in a meaningful and consistent way,
- *A business partner*: one with the skills she lacked – a professional actor and teacher,
- *Business acumen*: learned at Marks & Spencer UK, which had taught her the importance of customer relations, building a brand, and having a product that has quality and value,
- *An entrepreneurial spirit*: she had established several service projects in the community,
- *A desire to communicate* through the written word, publicity and messaging,
- *A sense of humor*: an invaluable business asset, and most important of all –
- *A "people first"* democratic perspective that encouraged others to join the endeavor and respected and honored their commitment and sought to incorporate their ideas.

This background is shared to boost the confidence of those who have a dream but think they don't have the necessary education, experience or skills to bring it to fruition. Just Do It!

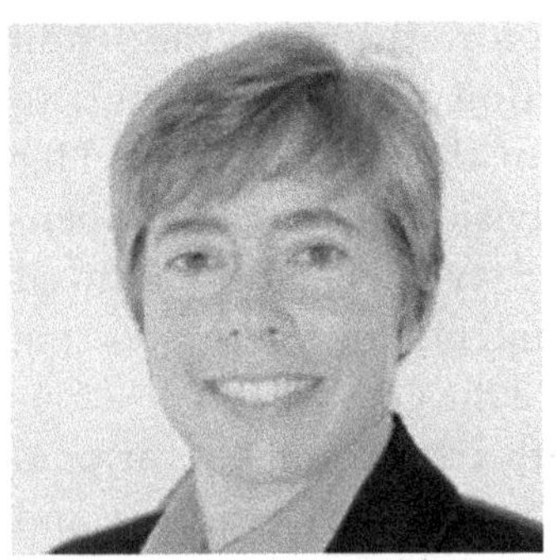

Brett Ashley Crawford.
Photograph by Peggy Thomas.

Brett Ashley Crawford (she/her) works at Carnegie Mellon University as an associate teaching professor and faculty chair of the arts and entertainment management programs, while also teaching theatre management for the School of Drama. Brett cannot deny that she is a lover of education and learning; she has an undergraduate degree in theatre from Northwestern University, an MFA in theatre management from Texas Tech University and a PhD in theatre history and criticism, plus a graduate certificate in women's studies from the University of Maryland, College Park. She has presented and lectured at dozens of conferences and universities, including Theatre Communications Group, the Association for Theatre in Higher Education, ENCATC, the Association for Performing Arts Presenters and the University of Helsinki. Her research and teaching focus on audiences, audience engagement, and social systems, particularly technology, and how it is disrupting our arts and cultural fields. She leads the Arts Management and Technology research center at Heinz College at CMU and she co-authored a book with Paul Hansen, *Raising the Curtain: Technology Success Stories from Performing Arts Leaders and Artists* (2024).

Her passion and life work has always been theatre. She began her career saying "yes" to every opportunity – from lighting design to working as a production assistant in film, but her strengths emerged as a creator (director, writer, marketer) and manager – stage manager and a member of Actors Equity Association, production manager, and managing director. She has worked on dozens of productions across her career and led three theatres as a managing director, with her last experience as managing director of Imagination Stage.

Her work with Imagination Stage began in 1999 when she stage-managed their annual gala event. At that time, it was a celebration of all things BAPA (Bethesda Academy of Performing Arts) and its professional theatre, Imagination Stage. There were 200 people backstage in a performance that offered a peak at the expansive impact the organization had in its work with families and children. She stage-managed two more galas, one in 2000 and one in 2005, the latter while still working as a professor at American University. In 2007, she joined the company full time first as director of education marketing and then as managing director.

www.ingramcontent.com/pod-product-compliance
Lightning Source LLC
Chambersburg PA
CBHW080913280825
31554CB00005B/8

* 9 7 8 1 8 3 5 9 5 1 2 2 4 *